Normalization of Violence

This book offers both a conceptual and an empirical analysis of how violence is normalized. In its conceptual analysis, Irm Haleem offers a framework of explanation that she argues is universal in its narratives, which she submits is premised on moralizing, legalizing, and popularizing violence. Haleem engages Stathis Kalyvas's notion of the two stages of violence (process and outcome), and proposes the notion of "metaphysical" violence as distinct from physical violence. Through drawing upon works of scholars such as Hannah Arendt, Noam Chomsky, W.J.T. Mitchell, Michel Foucault, Jacques Derrida, George Kateb, and others, she illustrates why these distinctions (of stages and types of violence) are critical in understanding how violence is normalized.

In its empirical analysis, Naoko Kumada argues that the contemporary changes in narratives and educational curriculum in Japan are intended to moralize the historic glory days of imperial Japan, which, she argues, may subsequently normalize militarism. Stefanie Kam focuses on how China has normalized violence in Xinjiang through narratives of the imperatives of security, thereby both legalizing and moralizing violence. Jennifer Dhanaraj argues how the denial of citizenship to the Rohingya community in Myanmar has provided both the moral and legal justifications for Buddhist extremists and the military to wage a brutal and unbridled war against the Rohingyas. Finally, Abdul Basit examines how the ex-communication of the Ahmadi sectarian minority in Pakistan has criminalized the minority, thus paving the way for unbridled violence against them from extremist mobs that have justified their violence in moral and legal terms. In all the cases in this book, we see how violence is popularized as being either a matter of the will of the people, or as being for the greater good of the people.

Irm Haleem is Assistant Professor in the Strategic Studies Program at S. Rajaratnam School of International Studies (RSIS), Nanyang Technological University (NTU) in Singapore, where she is also the Deputy Coordinator of MS (International Relations) Program at RSIS. Haleem received a PhD in Political Science from Boston University, and her work focuses on the conceptual study of violence. She is the author of the book *The Essence of Islamist Extremism: Recognition Through Violence, Freedom Through Death* (Routledge 2012, paperback 2014). She has taught at Northeastern University, Seton Hall University, and Princeton University.

Routledge Contemporary Asia Series

Protecting the Weak in East Asia
Framing, Mobilisation and Institutionalism
Edited by Iwo Amelung, Moritz Bälz, Heike Holbig, Matthias Schumann and Cornelia Storz

Middle Class, Civil Society and Democracy in Asia
Edited by Hsin-Huang Michael Hsiao

Conflict in India and China's Contested Borderlands
A Comparative Study
Kunal Mukherjee

Transcontinental Silk Road Strategies
Comparing China, Japan and South Korea in Uzbekistan
Timur Dadabev

Sino-Pakistani Relations
Politics, Military and Regional Dynamics
Filippo Boni

Circulation and Governance of Asian Medicine
Edited by Céline Coderey and Laurent Pordié

Normalization of Violence
Conceptual Analysis and Reflections from Asia
Edited by Irm Haleem

For more information about this series, please visit: www.routledge.com/Routledge-Contemporary-Asia-Series/book-series/SE0794

Normalization of Violence

Conceptual Analysis and Reflections from Asia

Edited by Irm Haleem

Routledge
Taylor & Francis Group
LONDON AND NEW YORK

First published 2020
by Routledge
2 Park Square, Milton Park, Abingdon, Oxon OX14 4RN

and by Routledge
52 Vanderbilt Avenue, New York, NY 10017

Routledge is an imprint of the Taylor & Francis Group, an informa business

First issued in paperback 2021

British Library Cataloguing-in-Publication Data
A catalogue record for this book is available from the British Library

Library of Congress Cataloging-in-Publication Data
A catalog record for this book has been requested

ISBN: 978-0-367-42329-2 (hbk)
ISBN: 978-1-03-208784-9 (pbk)
ISBN: 978-0-367-82359-7 (ebk)

Typeset in Times New Roman
by Apex CoVantage, LLC

Contents

Contributors

Abdul Basit is Associate Research Fellow (ARF) at the International Centre of Political Violence and Terrorism Research (ICPVTR) in S. Rajaratnam School of International Studies (RSIS), Nanyang Technological University in Singapore. He holds an MPhil in International Relations from Quaid-i-Azam University (QAU), Pakistan.

Jennifer Dhanaraj is a research analyst at *the International Centre of Political Violence and Terrorism Research* (ICPVTR) in S. Rajaratnam School of International Studies (RSIS), Nanyang Technological University (NTU) in Singapore. Her work focuses primarily on political violence and insurgencies in Southeast Asia. She is also an editor for ICPVTR's monthly *Counter Terrorist Trends* and *Analyst Journal*. Jennifer recently completed her Master's in International Relations with a specialization in terrorism studies at NTU.

Irm Haleem is Assistant Professor in the Strategic Studies Program at S. Rajaratnam School of International Studies (RSIS), Nanyang Technological University (NTU) in Singapore, where she is also the Deputy Coordinator of MS (International Relations) Program at RSIS. Haleem received a PhD in Political Science from Boston University, and her work focuses on the conceptual study of violence. She is the author of the book *The Essence of Islamist Extremism: Recognition through Violence, Freedom through Death* (Routledge 2012, paperback 2014). She has taught at Northeastern University, Seton Hall University, and Princeton University.

Stefanie Kam is a doctoral candidate at the National Security College, Australian National University. Prior to this, Stefanie was Associate Research Fellow at the S. Rajaratnam School of International Studies (RSIS), Nanyang Technological University in Singapore. Stefanie graduated in 2010 with an MA in Humanities from the University of Chicago and has an MSc in International Relations from RSIS, Nanyang Technological University.

Naoko Kumada is Visiting Scholar at the Weatherhead East Asian Institute, Columbia University, and Adjunct Fellow at S. Rajaratnam School of International Studies (RSIS), Nanyang Technological University (NTU) in Singapore, where she has focused her work on the politico-religious dimensions of Asian societies, particularly Japan and Burma. Prior to this, she taught at the Center for Buddhist Studies, Stanford University. She received a Bachelor of Laws degree from Keio University and completed her PhD in Social Anthropology on the religious practice of Burmese Buddhists at the University of Cambridge.

Preface

This book offers both a conceptual and an empirical analysis of how violence is normalized. In its conceptual analysis, the book draws upon works of prominent scholars such as Hannah Arendt, George Kateb, Stathis Kalyvas, Michel Foucault, Jacques Derrida, W.J.T. Mitchell, and Noam Chomsky, amongst others. In its empirical analysis, the book draws upon examples from Japan, China, Myanmar, and Pakistan. Nothing in this book is intended to suggest that the phenomenon of the normalization of violence is specific to Asia, much less to the countries examined in this book. On the contrary, as I discuss in the Introduction, Chapter One, and Conclusion of this book, the normalization of violence is both an existential and a universal phenomenon.

Acknowledgments

The journey of this book, from the point of the inception of the idea to the point of its consolidation, has been unusually complicated and complex. Throughout the process of the writing of this book, and of the eliciting of contributing authors, I received steadfast support from all the managers at the International Centre of Political Violence and Terrorism Research (ICPVTR), S. Rajarathnam School of International Studies (RSIS), Nanyang Technological University. In particular, I am grateful to Ambassador Ong Keng Yong for his steadfast support.

I am also most grateful to two other people at RSIS. First, Mr. Ali Marican Ansari (manager at ICPVTR), in whose office I casually coined the idea of this book in November 2016, and who encouraged me in various ways throughout the arduous process of getting an edited volume together. While I had initially imagined that the subject of the normalization of violence would comprise one of my single-authored books, it was Mr. Ansari who suggested that the treatment of the subject could be made richer if I were to invite other scholars to contribute to the volume. And, indeed, it must be said that the diversity of the cases covered in this volume could not have been a single-author endeavor.

And Dr. Ralf Emmers, Professor and Dean of RSIS, whose gentle but very convincing words of encouragement propelled me to take this volume to the finish line as expeditiously as possible. Thank you for your steadfast support!

My gratitude also goes to the anonymous reviewers, particularly "R1", whose detailed comments and questions were critical in refining this project and in more clearly delineating its aim and structure. Many thanks also to Simon Bates at Routledge, Singapore, who offered consistent support and understanding. Thank you for your words of encouragement!

Finally, it must be said that my gratitude also goes to Naoko Kumada, Stefanie Kam, Jennifer Dhanaraj, and Abdul Basit for their solid commitment to this volume, and for their incredible patience with the prolonged process of the consolidation of this volume. I am absolutely thrilled by all their unique and thoroughly researched analysis, and very proud to say: We made it!

Irm Haleem
Singapore, July 2019

Introduction to violence

Process, outcome, and types

Irm Haleem

The notion of the normalization of violence beckons a number of immediate questions: What is meant by normalization of violence, and normalization for whom? How and why is violence normalized? But, most fundamentally, what do we mean when we talk about violence? That is, what are the different types and stages of violence? In this Introduction, I address the more fundamental question of the meaning of "violence" and the different types and stages of violence, relegating the analysis of the meaning of "normalization of violence", and the analysis of the "how" and "why" of such normalization to Chapter One. Before proceeding with the question of the phenomenon of violence, some broad reflections on how violence has been explained and what are generally thought to be the causes of violence are in order.

Violence has been explained and justified in numerous ways. Some have explained violence as an existential phenomenon, intricately tied to human existence and its characteristic life-and-death struggles for recognition of the self, such that its absence is argued to mark the "end of history"—since history is peppered with instances of violence of greater or lesser degrees, such that a history without violence is both an anomaly and an oxymoron. Alexandre Kojeve's (1902–1968) notion of the 'end of history' forwards this very argument.[1] Others, however, have optimistically forecasted the very "end of history", challenging the notion that violence is integral to human existence. Francis Fukuyama's (1952–) post-cold war optimistic forecast as outlined in his article "The End of History?" forwards such an argument.[2] In contrast, violence has also been explained as a product of a "clash of civilizations"—a clash between western and eastern civilizations[3]—and as therefore inevitable and perpetual. Samuel Huntington's article "The Clash of Civilizations?" forwards such an argument.[4] In contrast to the notion of a clash of civilizations, others have explained violence as instead a reaction to colonialism, occupation, and oppression, and as neither a thing of the past, nor a product of ethno-religious identities.

Edward Said's (1935–2003) essay "The Clash of Ignorance" forwards such an argument by criticizing Huntington's monolithic understanding of cultures and ethnicities and his ethnocentric narratives of "the west, and the rest".[5] On similar critical grounds, Noam Chomsky (1928–) argues that the notion of the clash of civilizations offers but a new justification to the western powers for their continued militaristic policies, especially in light of the demise of their traditional justifications that were premised on superpowers' cold war politics.[6] There are also those who have explained violence as a product of modernity, leading to unconventional and "invisible" manifestations of violence. Zygmunt Bauman and Leonidas Donskis, in their book *Liquid Evil*, forward such an argument.[7] Modernity, they claim, has robbed the sense of unity amongst humans and replaced it with "forced individualism" which encourages unconventional forms of violence, but which also makes violence invisible as it becomes more ordinary and smaller in scale, yet nonetheless abundant and perpetual.

Beyond macro explanations of violence—as outlined previously—micro explanations of violence tend to focus on a number of variables: economic, social, and political inequalities; policies or events that aggravate already existing economic, social, or political grievances; racial or religious prejudice; ultra-nationalistic groups or movements; and psychological factors such as childhood abuse or psychopathic pathologies. The causes of violence are often understood as synonymous to motivations of violence. But this tendency is problematic as "motivations" may be a product of a number of "causes" that intertwine to ultimately generate (physical) violence. For example, Stathis Kalyvas argues that

> individual motivations of violence may mix hatred (of many sorts), peer pressure (Browning 1992), obedience (Milgram 1974), honor, rituals, and collective imaginaries (Nahoum-Grappe 1996; Zemon Davis 1973), greed (Paul and Demarest 1988), revenge (Frijda 1994), or sadistic impulses; they may also result from the consumption of alcohol (Tishkov 2004: 139); G. Jones 1989: 124) or the use of drugs (Aussaresses 2001; Peters and Richards 1998).[8]

Anatomy of violence: stages and types

Stathis Kalyvas's book, *The Logic of Violence in Civil War*, has been critically acclaimed as essential reading for matters related to violence in general, and civil war violence in particular. Kalyvas offers a dense and stratified analysis of violence, breaking it down into different stages, while primarily focusing exclusively on physical violence. His analysis of physical violence identifies different motivations and desired outcomes for (physical) violence.[9]

In the reminder of this section, I discuss stages and types of violence. First, I discuss Kalyvas's notion of the stages of violence as being divided into "process" and "outcome", and the criticality of understanding this distinction in order to understand the dynamics that lead to the normalization of violence. Second, I discuss types of violence, wherein I propose a category of violence that I refer to as "metaphysical violence". I argue that metaphysical violence can be understood in the context of Kalyvas's "process" of violence, and that therefore metaphysical violence precedes physical violence, just as "process" precedes "outcome" of violence.

Stages of violence: process versus outcome

Stathis Kalyvas distinguishes two stages of violence: process and outcome. He argues that as a process, violence involves more than just aggressors and victims. It involves collaborators and sympathizers who are complicit in the events, mass mobilization, narrative acceptance and dissemination, and the politics and policies that eventually lead to physical violence. In other words, violence as a process describes those "sequence of decisions and events that intersect to produce violence".[10] Kalyvas argues that the collaborators and sympathizers that are central to the process of violence are often invisible and informal—that is, they are not necessarily members of a government, but 'regular people' that form the populace (the masses) and that play a crucial role in ultimately supporting and thus legitimizing violence. On the other hand, he notes that violence as an outcome is tangible and physical, and comprises only aggressors and victims, even if the distinction between victims and aggressors often gets blurred in reality.

In underscoring the importance of the distinction between process and outcome, Kalyvas argues that any analysis of violence that doesn't recognize these two components (of process and outcome) as distinct phenomenon *within* the larger phenomenon of violence only generates a reductionist understanding of the dynamics of violence as it fails to recognize the critical component of violence in the making (the process of violence). Conceivably, then, we might argue that recognizing the critical stage of the process of violence might put us in the position to retard this process—which comprises narrative creation and dissemination—before it leads to its outcome of physical violence, with its characteristic downward spiral of action-reaction dynamic, which, once unleashed, is hard to control.[11] But, Kalyvas notes that even more important than recognizing violence as comprising two distinct stages of process and outcome is recognizing the fact that both process and outcome can—and often do—exist simultaneously with each other. This makes sense as while the process of violence is necessary to create the narratives for the justifications of violence that ultimately legitimize violence as a physical outcome, continued supplementation of these narratives is necessary to breathe new life into the legitimacy of the ongoing physical violence.

Types of violence: metaphysical versus physical

In his discussion of violence, Kalyvas focuses on physical violence but recognizes that there are other, non-physical types of violence, such as psychological violence. In this section, I offer a categorization of all types of non-physical in terms of what I call 'metaphysical' violence. I argue that metaphysical violence may include psychological violence, but also other forms of non-physical violence, such as narratives that manufacture enemies and that manufacture the consent for violence against those designated as enemies. In other words, I contend that metaphysical violence can be understood as the building blocks, if you may, that justify and legitimize physical violence and that therefore ultimately lead to physical violence. Metaphysical violence can thus be understood in terms of what Kalyvas describes as the 'process' of violence. Since the direction of causation flows from metaphysical violence to physical violence, I address metaphysical violence first before addressing physical violence.

Metaphysical violence

Metaphysical violence is non-physical, intangible violence—hence 'metaphysical', or beyond the physical. By 'intangible violence' I mean those explanations and justifications of violence that ultimately legitimize and thus normalize physical violence. Metaphysical violence is then the 'process' of violence. However, in diverging from Kalyvas's contention, I argue that the process of violence itself has different stages *within* the process. And these different stages within the process of violence include not only narrative creation, but also narrative dissemination. Understanding how violence is normalized requires, I argue, an understanding of the different stages *within* the process of violence, or the different manifestations of metaphysical violence. Chapter One offers a more detailed analysis of these stages *within* the process of violence. In the reminder of this section, however, I more broadly introduce the different components of metaphysical violence, leaving a more detailed analysis to Chapter One.

1 *Language of Violence*—The language of violence is premised not only on otherizing the other, but also on narratives that portray the other as

"filthy", "evil", and "dangerous". The language of violence thus describes the narratives that moralize, legalize, and popularize violence, and that therefore normalize violence. Metaphors in such narratives, or hate-speech, rely on racial, gender, religious, and cultural stereotypes that not only invoke fear and disgust, but also indirectly equate the "other" to an inferior being, and the self to a "superior" being. And such notions of inferiority and superiority further normalize violence as they pit the self as the "moral" and "righteous" being where even the violence one uses becomes framed as "necessary" and "moral", and the other as "immoral" and "profane". All violence incited by such narratives then fundamentally becomes justified as the "right thing to do". The language of violence, then, in creating narratives of violence, essentially manufactures enemies.

2 *Iconography*—Iconography functions as an effective visual dissemination of the narratives of violence, but also, therefore, as a narrative itself. Iconography may be merely cultural or inflammatory. I submit that cultural iconography merely offers an insight into the culture and sensibility of a people in any given time and space, and, as such, is harmless. Inflammatory iconography, however, intends to promote or provoke violence through visuals that are intended to frighten its audiences and thus to promote harm to the designated enemy. Ample examples can be cited of inflammatory iconography. Consider, for example, the derogatory portrayals of Jews as grotesque, gigantic beings bent on violence, as seen in medieval European anti-Jewish iconography.[12] Such anti-Jewish iconographies seem very clearly intended not only to otherize the Jews as demonic or deformed beings distinct from other Europeans, but also therefore to incite *defensive* violence against them. Consider also the derogatory images of Israeli Jews as blood-sucking demons, serpents, or pigs and monkeys as presented in murals, leaflets, and other publications sponsored by HAMAS (an acronym of *Ḥarakat al-Muqāwamah al-ʾIslāmiyyah*, or Islamic Resistance Movement) in Gaza and the West Bank. Such inflammatory iconography seems very clearly intended to dehumanize the Israelis and thus justify and incite violence in the form of terrorism against them. Iconography, then, in disseminating narratives of violence, essentially manufactures consent for the use of violence against the designated enemy.

3 *Psychological Violence*—Beyond narratives of violence (both language and iconography), we may also consider psychological violence as a category of metaphysical violence. Psychological violence qualifies as metaphysical violence as it is predicated on power play (intimidation and manipulation) and therefore on the *threat* of the use of force and violence, and not on actual use of (physical) violence. On a macro level we might understand cold war brinkmanship of the United States

and the former Soviet Union as a classic example, and on the micro level we might consider honor codes[13] and blasphemy laws[14] as classic examples. In both these macro and micro examples, violence is threatened or implied as a punitive *reaction* to violations of political, social, or religious protocols or codes of behavior, but not necessarily used. However, to the extent that psychological violence is not a product of the manufacturing of enemies—unlike narratives of violence—but instead a tactic of intimidation against already manufactured enemies, the category of psychological violence proves irrelevant to the discussion of the normalization of violence.

Physical violence

In his analysis of physical violence, Kalyvas distinguishes four subcategories: intentional, unintentional, indiscriminate, and selective. Furthermore, he distinguishes between "violence that preserves the social order ('systemically functional' violence) and violence that destroys it ('dysfunctional' violence)".[15] Given these distinctions, we might understand defensive violence as violence that seeks to preserve order, and thus as "systemically functional" violence. In contrast, we might understand revolutions, insurgencies, and terrorism as violence that seeks to destroy the social order, and as thus "dysfunctional" violence. Of course, as with any categorizations or discussions related to violence, the categories of 'systemically functional' violence and "dysfunctional violence" are decidedly subjective. What may be perceived as functional to one person may be seen as dysfunctional to another.

Still, there is undoubtedly much credibility in these categorizations. Take the example of international war as a defensive measure. If the sovereign integrity of a particular country comes under attack, from either an invasion by a neighboring country or by transnational terrorism, then violence that is engaged in by the country under attack can be seen as violence for the ends of preserving order, or the status quo of the integrity of its sovereign borders. On the other hand, violence as the outcome of revolutions, insurgencies, and terrorism is, by definition, violence intended to change the status quo. The status quo here may be understood broadly as the actual or perceived injustices for which masses are mobilized in the form of revolution, or specific sectors of a population in the form of insurgencies or terrorism. After all, revolutionaries seek a complete overhaul of the political, economic, and social structure of their society; insurgents seek retribution, accountability, and preferably an overthrow of their own government; and terrorists seeks a change in the domestic or international political order to one that recognizes them as significant players.

But whether violence is intended to preserve order or to disrupt or destroy it, Kalyvas argues that physical violence (or violence as an outcome) may be divided into four additional subcategories: indiscriminate, selective, intentional, or unintentional. Violence of terrorist groups may be accurately understood as indiscriminate as it does not selectively target victims but indiscriminately targets all those present in the area where either a bomb is detonated or where a suicide bomber activates his or her bomb device. On the other hand, violence of insurgent groups may be understood as targeted as insurgents often select high-profile targets, such as government or military institutions, and not society at large as their grievances rest squarely with their selective targets. Violence of both terrorist groups and insurgents can be understood as intentional, whereas violence that inadvertently ends up harming bystanders at a protest, for example, can be understood as unintentional violence. The collateral damage caused to bystanders in insurgencies may also be viewed as unintentional violence as the targets of insurgents are specific and not the general public.

Chapter layout

The chapters in this book are organized along the lines of the three broad categories of the narratives of violence that I introduce in Chapter One: moralizing violence, legalizing violence, and popularizing violence. I submit that all violence is justified along the lines of one or more of these three categories such that we may understand these broad categories as comprising universal justifications of violence, conceptually speaking. In Chapter One, then, I lay out the conceptual framework for how violence is normalized, not only along the lines of these three-pronged categories of the narratives of violence, but also along the lines of the methods for narrative dissemination. This chapter therefore focuses on the process of violence and, as such, on what I call metaphysical violence. Chapters Two, Three, Four, and Five offer empirical analysis of the normalization of violence that illustrates the concurrent nature of the process and outcome of violence. As such, these chapters discuss the narratives of violence alongside the outcome of violence as seen in China, Myanmar, and Pakistan. The chapter on Japan, however, offers an interesting case as it exhibits a sophisticated process of violence but with a complete absence of violence as outcome. In other words, while all other chapters illustrate how narratives of violence (violence as process) translate into incidences of violence (violence as outcome), the Japan chapter only illustrates narratives of violence that are presumably prepping the society for future militarism, and thus violence as outcome.

In Chapter One, *How Violence Iis Normalized: On the Process of Violence*, I focus on the process of violence, and the two stages *within* the process of violence: narratives of violence, and the dissemination of the narratives of violence. In this chapter I argue that the narratives of violence, conceptually speaking, are universal. As such, all narratives of violence seek to moralize, legalize, and popularize violence. I submit that the tools for the dissemination of these narratives are also universal in that they rely on the common discourse dissemination outlets (such as media of sorts) and iconography. Drawing upon George Kateb, I argue that the narratives of violence focus on *manufacturing enemies*; while drawing upon Noam Chomsky, I argue that the dissemination of narratives focuses on *manufacturing consent* for violence. And it is these two elements, functioning in tandem with each other, that, I argue, normalizes violence.

In Chapter Two, *Moralizing Militarism through Educational Curriculum in Japan*, Naoko Kumada begins her analysis from the era of World War II, when the Imperial Shinto state unleashed violence that cost the lives of 20 million victims in Asia. She argues that the political theology of the time, invented after the Meiji Restoration (1868), constructed Japan as a theocratic nation. The idea of Japan as a theocratic nation was inculcated through a curriculum of 'moral' education that trained children to hold as their highest value the sacrifice of their lives for the Emperor. Thus, the Meiji oligarchs developed Japanese nationalism by constructing a Shinto theocracy that combined Japan's *previously separate* civil and religious powers in the person of a deified Emperor. Combined with militarism, Kumada argues that this made for an especially extreme form of nationalism. The post-war national legislature, however, invalidated the pre-war 'moral' education as being incompatible with the new pacifist Constitution's principles of human rights and popular sovereignty. However, Kumada argues that today this pre-war 'moral' education is being revived, as the Abe administration pushes educational reforms. Kumada ultimately argues that this revival must be critically examined in the historical context of Shinto nationalism and its consequent ultra-nationalist outcomes. While the government moves constitutional reforms to pave the way for the re-arming of Japan, educational reforms are drawing once more on the ideology of wartime Japan. Kumada asserts that, therefore, we are observing a shift in the post-war Japanese nationalism, and the resurgence of religious nationalism of a peculiarly total character. It is these developments, she argues, which will ultimately normalize militarism, and, subsequently, any violence associated with that in the future.

In Chapter Three, *China's Security Imperatives and Violence in Xinjiang*, Stefanie Kam argues that the processes of securitization in the Xinjiang Uyghur Autonomous Regime (XUAR) have largely become normalized through the state's legal and moral justification for its policies since the 1980s. Kam argues that the legal imperatives can be seen with respect to China's institutionalization of counterterrorism institutions, operations, and policies; while the moral imperatives can be seen in the use of religious, cultural, and social controls in Xinjiang province. This, she argues, is consistent with Michel Foucault's notion of pastoral power. Pastoral power, she elaborates, is embedded in these moral imperatives which inculcate a sense that the state's functioning of power are, in fact, practices of 'care' and that the Han Chinese and the 55 other ethnic minority groups, including the Uyghurs, must defer to state imperatives of security for their own welfare and security, or be punished for their disobedience. In her chapter, Kam provides an overview of the history of Uyghur rebellions in Xinjiang from the early 20th century to the 1990s, which she argues informs the state's perceptions of the threat. In her analysis of the Chinese normalization of violence, Kam reflects on the implications for China's management of the Uyghur ethnic minority in the Xinjiang region.

In Chapter Four, *From Pacifism to Violence in Buddhist Myanmar*, Jennifer Dhanaraj examines the case of the Myanmar government and its denial of citizenship to the Rohingya community. Dhanaraj notes that this denial is further codified in the exclusion of the Rohingya community from the 2014 census. She argues that this exclusion propagates the narrative that the Rohingya Muslims are in fact "the other", and thus it signals to Buddhist extremist groups that any violence perpetrated against "the other" will be justified as moral and necessary. Violence against the Rohingyas is further normalized, she contends, through the government's consistent refusal to acknowledge the military's role in the ethnic cleansing campaign against Rohingya Muslims. As such, the military continues to perpetuate false narratives about the Rohingya as a threat and as the other. Dhanaraj notes that as recently as August 2018, a new book written on the Rohingya by the army's department of public relations and psychological warfare rewrote key aspects of history to justify the killings of Rohingyas. By constructing the narrative that Rohingya Muslims are the other, which extends to Muslims across Myanmar, the Myanmar government has succeeded in fueling mistrust between the two religions. Dhanaraj notes that the government has in fact failed to take a stronger stance against violent Buddhist extremists, further contributing to the normalization of violence.

In Chapter Five, *Legalization of Violence against the Pakistani Ahmadis*, Abdul Basit examines the legal justifications that provide frameworks for violence against the Ahmadis, a sectarian minority in the country. He argues that such violence is normalized in Pakistan through government policies that excommunicate and criminalize the sectarian practices of the Ahmadis. As a result, the Ahmadis have encountered various forms of violence, political discrimination, and social ostracization in Pakistan. Basit analyzes the legal frameworks that have produced, sustained, and reinforced these social and ideological prejudices against the Ahmadis. He notes that the violence against the Ahmadis has been normalized to such an extent that killing of the Ahmadis is considered fair game that no longer raises eyebrows. Furthermore, he notes that various Pakistani governments have appeased the radical Islamists by passing anti-Ahmadi laws to bolster their ideological legitimacy, and to also neutralize political competition from the extremists. This has allowed the radical Islamist groups to increase their influence in the society with catastrophic effects for country's inter-faith and intra-faith harmony.

Notes

1 Kojeve's argument of the inevitability of violence, and its absence as being akin to the 'end of history', is premised on a Hegelian argument of the existentiality of life-and-death struggles for recognition of the self. See Alexandre Kojeve, *Introduction to the Reading of Hegel: Lectures on the Phenomenology of Spirit*, assembled by Raymond Queneau, edited by Allan Bloom, translated by James H. Nichols, Jr. (Ithaca: Cornell University Press, 1969). Other scholars who have drawn upon the Hegelian notion of struggles for recognition as an explanation of violence include Franz Fanon (*The Wretched of the Earth*, 1961), Charles Taylor (*Multiculturalism: Examining the Politics of Recognition*, 1994), Axel Honneth (*Struggles for Recognition: The Moral Grammar of Social Conflicts*, 1995), and Irm Haleem (*The Essence of Islamist Extremism: Recognition through Violence, Freedom through Death*, 2012), amongst others.

2 See Francis Fukuyama, "The End of History?", *The National Interest*, no. 16 (Summer 1989), pp. 3–18.

3 Huntington's work offers more complicated categories than just 'western' and 'eastern', but my intention here is just to offer a very preliminary brushstroke explanation of the 'clash of civilizations' as a more detailed analysis is not the subject of this chapter.

4 Samuel Huntington, "The Clash of Civilizations?", *Foreign Affairs*, vol. 72, no. 3 (Summer 1993), pp. 22–49. Of note is the fact that the term 'clash of civilizations' is not itself attributed to Huntington alone, as others had utilized this expression before him, such as Albert Camus (1946), Girilal Jian (1988), and Bernard Lewis (1990), to name a few.

5 See Edward Said, "The Clash of Ignorance", *The Nation* (October 22, 2001).

6 See Noam Chomsky's response to the question of whether Taliban-US conflict in 2001 was a clash of civilizations in "India 2001: A Symposium on the Year That Was", www.india-seminar.com/2002/509.htm.

7 See Zygmunt Bauman and Leonidas Donskis, *Liquid Evil* (Cambridge, UK: Polity Press, 2016).

8 Stathis Kalyvas, *The Logic of Violence in Civil War* (New York: Cambridge University Press, 2006), 24–25. All in-text citations appear in Kalyvas's original text and were not added by myself.

9 Kalyvas also identifies situations where violence would not be desired; however, a comprehensive analysis of the different scenarios of violence is beyond the scope of this chapter.

10 Kalyvas, *The Logic of Violence in Civil War*, 22.

11 Kalyvas also distinguishes between war and violence in war; see Kalyvas, *The Logic of Violence in Civil War*, 20. A discussion of this distinction, however, is beyond the scope of this book.
12 See, for example, Sara Lipton, *Dark Mirror: The Medieval Origins of Anti-Jewish Iconography* (New York: Metropolitan Books, 2014).
13 It is interesting to note that medieval Europe was rife with strict honor codes for society, the violation of which could literally result in the cutting of the nose for women, or "the loss of two fingers of their right hand" for men, as punishment for fornication and adultery. See Valentin Groebner, *Defaced: The Visual Culture of Violence in the Late Middle Ages* (New York: Zone Books, 2004), 77, 77–86 for the larger discussion of gendered honor-related punishments.
14 It is important to acknowledge that it is not merely Muslim countries that sport blasphemy laws. For example, Austria, Brazil, Germany, and Italy are countries that are not normally associated with blasphemy laws but that have blasphemy laws in their penal codes; while Iran, Pakistan, and Saudi Arabia are countries that are not commonly associated with blasphemy laws, and commonly cited as such, and have blasphemy laws in their penal codes.
15 Kalyvas, *The Logic of Violence in Civil War*, 19.

1 How violence is normalized

On the process of violence

Irm Haleem

Violence is normalized when it is no longer viewed as immoral or unconscionable, but as instead moral and ordinary. When this happens, all forms of violence, regardless of their monstrosity and inhumanity, become accepted as simply matters of routine behavior. I submit that one of the reasons why the American military's reference to "Standard Operating Procedures" to describe its various actions in its "war on terror" has been so offensive is precisely because such "standard procedures" have come to describe actions such as psychological torture and drone warfare, actions wherein either innocent individuals were victims or where international standards of proportionality were violated.[1] The reference to standard operating procedures, therefore, essentially normalized any atrocities committed under its banner. It is such normalization of violence and brutality that concerned Hannah Arendt in her analysis of the monstrosities of both Stalin and Hitler's regimes, and it is this very concern that formed the basis of her notion of the "banality of evil", and that forms the basis of this chapter.[2]

Although Arendt was centrally concerned with how ideology and terror operates to create compliant and complicit masses in brutal totalitarian regimes, it was not until the trial of the former Nazi SS-Kommandant,[3] Adolf Eichmann, in Jerusalem in 1961 that she refined her notion of the banality of evil.[4] In understanding the factors that contributed to Adolf Eichmann's brutal complicity with the Nazi regime, Arendt points to "his acceptance of the idea . . . that mass killing represented a heroic task requiring great courage", and the "different personal attitude" that Eichmann adopted after witnessing the death of masses of people.[5] It is the *acceptance* of the *idea* of violence that is critical here. This is because such an acceptance is fundamentally premised on the *deconstruction* (reconceptualization) of the notions of morality and legality, so that what was once considered immoral and illegal now becomes considered moral and legal. Factors such as selfish calculations of the desire for promotion and recognition within the ranks of the Nazi Party were, argues Arendt, central to Eichmann's complicity with Nazi monstrosity. Arendt observes:

> It is of great political interest to know how long it takes an average person to overcome his innate repugnance toward crime, and what exactly happens to him once he has reached that point. . . . Yes, he [Eichmann] had a conscience, and his conscience functioned in the expected way for about four weeks, whereupon it began to function the other way around.[6]

The point of Eichmann's turnaround, notes Arendt, was the point wherein he saw the brutality that he was complicit in as not only normal and routine, but as in fact moral and even as *categorically imperative*—I analyze Eichmann's deconstructive reason in a little more detail later in this chapter.

Arendt's notion of the banality of evil has been the subject of much misunderstanding, the starkest of which misunderstands the notion as meaning that the evils committed by the Nazi regime were "ordinary" in the sense of being unremarkable. Ironically, it is this very misunderstanding that explains the dynamics of Arendt's notion of the banality of evil, namely that it is precisely the *human tendency* to accept wholesale the narratives that have been constructed by authority, unquestionably and uncritically, that leads to their acceptance as ordinary, routine, and even moral. George Kateb explains this very fine distinction in a sharply astute manner as thus:

> Arendt's hard truth, perhaps her hardest truth, is that when many if not most awful events in political life happen, not only the evil of totalitarianism, the leading perpetrators do not feel, as, say, Macbeth does, that they are doing or even intending wrong; rather, they usually think sincerely that they are serving a mission of some kind.[7]

In other words, the "ordinariness" of violence and brutality is achieved through an uncritical acceptance of duty and orders to the point that the individual carrying out those orders or duty does not *perceive* themselves as evil or bad, but as moral and good. That is, unlike Macbeth, who knew he was evil and reveled in that fact, the banal individual accepts narratives of violence so wholeheartedly that they do not even recognize that they have become evil; in order words, the very fact of their own monstrosity escapes them! This tendency for self-deception becomes more potent and damning because, notes Arendt, there exists a human "proclivity to become enclosed in ideologies or fiction".[8]

Before proceeding further, some important points that were outlined in the previous chapter need to be restated here. First, narratives that normalize violence are universally premised on moralizing, legalizing, and popularizing violence. Such narratives of violence essentially describe what Stathis Kalyvas refers to as the "process" of violence. The process of violence, as I outlined in the previous chapter, is that stage before violence actually manifests itself physically. Second, narratives that normalize violence describe that process of violence where narratives are created, disseminated, and uncritically accepted by the populace (the masses). Third, the populace becomes an integral component of the process of violence as its uncritical acceptance of the narratives of violence functions to facilitate (legitimize) the narratives of the elites (those in positions of political, economic, or military power). So the process of violence, as Kalyvas notes, describes all those who facilitate and collaborate in the process that ultimately results in physical violence. Fourth, the process of violence, as thus outlined, describes the type of violence that is non-physical, what I refer to as "metaphysical violence" (as introduced in the Introduction). And it is this process of violence that is critical in not only normalizing violence, but also in understanding how violence is normalized. This chapter is thus an analysis of the process of violence that functions to normalize violence. And this process of violence, I argue, comprises the narratives of violence (moralizing, legalizing, and popularizing violence) as well as the effective dissemination of these narratives of violence (through media, speeches, declarations, and iconography).

Narratives of violence: manufacturing enemies

George Kateb points out that in her analysis of totalitarianism, Hannah Arendt focused specifically on the "attractiveness of mental constructions—especially ideologies—that reduce reality to an all-encompassing story or picture, that are revered or idealized as the *truth* about reality or some higher reality, and that are cartoon-like and ruinously untrue to reality".[9] He notes that these ideologies—narratives—become all the more destructive not only because "they promise harm to designated enemies", but because they are in fact "built on the *manufacture of enemies*".[10] The notion of the "enemy", therefore, is not only constructed and variable, but also subjective and reflective of the specific political agenda of the narrative creators at any given time. Quite simply, this means that anyone can be designated as the "enemy", and when designated as such, any violent action taken against them as "enemy" can be framed in moral, legal, and imperative terms.

The phenomenon of the production of narratives that manufactures enemies can best be understood in the context of what Stathis Kalyvas calls the "process of violence", which I introduced in the Introduction. In other words, the production and dissemination of narratives is that part of the dynamics of violence where there are more actors involved than merely victims and aggressors; there are also collaborators and facilitators who largely remain invisible. Kalyvas notes that these invisible actors are as much responsible for the *outcome* of violence (its physical manifestation) as are those who directly engage in acts of physical violence (mobs, soldiers, insurgents, counterinsurgents, and terrorists).

Arendt's notion of the banality of evil does not only explain the human tendency to uncritically accept narratives and orders, but it also, therefore, sheds light on the dynamics of mass society. Salvador Giner explains mass society as one where critical thinking is abandoned in the interests of mass thinking, and where individuality is abandoned in the interests of "mass man".[11] Giner credits Jose Ortega "for the origins of the term mass man",[12] and notes that according to Ortega, mass man has the following universal characteristics: he is average, in the sense that he has a mentality to want to be part of the collective; he is conformist, because he is vulnerable and in search of a sense of identity; he is vulgar in that he believes that "to be different is to be indecent"; he is a dominant man, in the sense that his banality is the norm, and thus he is common and "dominant" in the sense that there are many such as him, but also in the sense that he revels in the ability to dominate "minorities"; he is self-content in the sense that he sees his conformity as a matter of pride and as thus a basis for his arrogance; he is barbaric in that he revels in invading, dominating, and destroying and in fact uses these actions not only to define himself, but to draw a sense of self-worth from them.[13]

The wholesale and uncritical acceptance of narratives of violence can also be understood in the context of Stanley Milgram's celebrated work on conformity that, in his own description of his work, sought to establish the contemporary relevance of Hannah Arendt's notion of the banality of evil. Through a series of experiments conducted at Yale University in the 1960s, Milgram drew two main conclusions: (1) people have a tendency to obey orders if they think that the orders are coming from someone they recognize as a legitimate authority; and (2) people are even remarkably comfortable in inflicting pain on others if they think that they are obeying legitimate orders, and therefore feel that they are doing the right thing.[14] Following in Milgram's footsteps, Philip Zimbardo conducted his own version of an experiment at Stanford University in 1971, wherein he recruited a group of male college students and assigned them the roles of prisoners and prison guards, acting in a mock prison setting. The outcomes of this experiment was shocking in that within only a few days, the prison guards played by the otherwise seemingly good-natured students turned tyrannical and sadistic. As a result of this experiment, that went awry within just a few days, Zimbardo coined the term "the Lucifer effect": the situation where good people do bad things.[15]

In the reminder of this section, I analyze three ways in which reason and reality are constructed and deconstructed, thereby manufacturing enemies and encouraging the banality of evil: moralizing violence, legalizing violence, and popularizing violence.

Moralizing violence

One of the most universal ways in which violence is *moralized*, even in its extreme forms of brutality and monstrosity, is through contextualizing such violence within religious texts and tenets. In so doing, violence is framed not as an atrocity, but as Divine will, and, as such, both necessary and morally imperative. The tendency to use religious tenets as justifications for violence is so universal that there exists Sociological, Philosophical, Anthropological, Psychological, and Political Science studies to analyze this very instrumentality of religion. This instrumentality can be understood in very basic terms as the universal tendency to link religion with morality.

David Frankfurter explains the link between religion and violence through a two-fold logic: the construction of evil, and the deconstruction of evil.[16] He argues that images and narratives create a myth of evil that is at once based on demonizing the other (constructing evil) while glorifying the self. The other—the other religious, ethnic, cultural, or racial group—is demonized through framing their ways of being as savage, monstrous, immoral, and barbaric. In contrast, the self is presented as moral, civil, and godly. In other words, the construction of evil is a two-sided coin: on the one side, the other is constructed as evil; on the other side, all actions taken by the self, even violent and brutal actions, are *deconstructed* as moral, necessary, and imperative.

James Jones draws upon Stanley Milgram, Philip Zimbardo, and Scott Atran to offer a psychological and ethnopolitical explanation that focuses not only on group but also individual dynamics to explain the phenomenon of religion and violence:

> Individual psychopathology is rarely an explanation; that the experience of humiliation is often a precursor to violence; that *religiously motivated terrorist groups share common themes regardless of tradition*; that previously the leader-follower dynamic appeared crucial for turning a group violent, but understanding contemporary "leaderless" groups may require different models; that understanding the psychology of apocalyptic theologies is important.[17]

Jones's argument of the different models that may be required to understand the leaderless incidences of violence and terrorism—popularly known as "lone wolf" terrorism—is an important one. I submit that this model could draw upon the theory of recognition, as articulated historically by the

German philosopher G.W.F. Hegel, but as further elaborated by contemporary scholars such as Frantz Fanon, Axel Honneth, and Charles Taylor, and others.

In fact, I have argued elsewhere that the essence of Islamist extremism can best be understood in the context of a Hegelian life-and-death struggle for recognition.[18] The desire for recognition, it must be noted, operates on several levels: individual, social, and state. In the case of Islamist extremist groups with hierarchical power structures, it is a social recognition that is sought, wherein identification with, and conformity to, a group is critical. However, in the case of lone-wolf Islamist extremists, it is an individual recognition that is sought, wherein the identification and conformity is not to a group per se, but to an ideology, as in, for example, the ideology of the Islamic State.

The criticality of ideology in constructing narratives of violence is at least as important as context-specific experiences that give life to narratives of violence. For example, in addressing the question of the link between religion and violence, John Hall argues that it is not religion, categorically speaking, that can be held responsible for promoting violence, any more than it can be held completely inconsequential to promoting violence. And so, argues Hall, the three common views linked to the question of religion and violence are all faulty: religion is not at all to blame; religion is all to blame; and religion is not to blame, as the problem is simply the politicization of religion. Hall argues instead for a "synthetic theoretical account" for understanding this link.

Hall's synthetic theoretical account requires some familiarity with epistemology. Epistemologists argue that knowledge of reality is either based on experience or reason. Knowledge based on experience alone is referred to as *a posteriori* knowledge or judgment, while knowledge based on reason alone is referred to as *a priori* knowledge or judgment. Some clarification on the experience of "experience" is needed here. Experience may be based on our observations, our memory of the observations, and the manner in which we categorize and systemize that experience in our minds (the cognitive element of experience). For example, a soldier's experience of combat, his memory of that experience, and what he made of that experience varies from soldier to soldier. This means that two people can experience the same thing but make different sense of it.

But experience, notes Anil Gupta, also includes historical narratives that one chooses to accept, in addition to personal experience and the memory of such experience.[19] The phenomenon of experience is, therefore, decidedly subjective and variable. In contrast, knowledge based on reason can be of two sorts: knowledge based on pure reason that "creates" a *new* understanding of reality, and is thus *synthetic a priori*; and knowledge based on *analytical truths* wherein the truth (fact) is implied *within* the predicate of a statement. An example of an analytical truth may be a statement such as "Josh is a bachelor"; this is because the word "bachelor", by definition, means unmarried, so the truth of Josh's marital status is implied within the statement without explicitly noting that he is married. *Synthetic a priori* statements, much like *synthetic a posteriori* statements, are variable and subjective: the former because it is based on variable reason, the latter because it is based on variable experience. However, *analytical truths* are not variable or subjective, unless of course we wish to debate the meaning of the word "bachelor" in the example I've given earlier.[20]

There are two critical implications arising out of the epistemological distinctions that I have sketched previously. First, since experience is subjective, knowledge based on experience (a posteriori judgment) yields *contingent* knowledge; that is, knowledge that is contingent on one's experience and one's particular interpretation of that experience (one's cognitive categorizing and systemizing of that experience). This means that a posteriori knowledge is *contingent synthetic* knowledge: it is contingent on a particular experience of a particular person and their interpretation of the experience, and it is therefore *synthetic* as it is a *creation* of sorts, and not a universal truth. Second, knowledge based on pure reason (*a priori* judgment)—not analytical truths (*a priori* but analytically true)—is also *synthetic* but *a priori*, and therefore subjective and variable but based on reason not experience.[21] Or, to put it simply, Hall argues that it is the particular *experiences*—which are contextually, temporally, and individually variable—that determines whether religion becomes associated with violence. A good experience with religion delinks this causality; a bad experience does the opposite.

Having discussed the universal tendency to moralize violence by contextualizing it in religious narratives, I would be remiss if I did not also acknowledge the secular venue wherein violence is moralized. The construction of the narratives of violence as morality is also aided by framing violence as a means to a moral end. Consider, for example, the official US government narrative of its "war on terror" as "Operation Enduring Freedom". Here, war is not just about the destruction of the enemy, it is also about delivering the people in the enemy's domain from servitude and unfreedoms, to a better state of being: an existence with freedom. Beyond framing one's own actions (namely, American actions) in moral consequentialist terms—as the needed means for the ends of self-defense and recourse to terrorism—this narrative, I argue, also implicitly suggests that we (Americans) are big enough to rise above our own pain of being attacked on 9/11 to actually caring about the wellbeing of the people in enemy states, through liberating them from the shackles of tyranny, albeit through occupation and thus through violence and war.

Legalizing violence

The dogmatic, subjective, and self-righteous nature of notions of morality lends itself to the tendency to be converted into matters of legality, into matters of codes of public behavior enforced though punitive sanctions. Notions of morality, then, as disseminated by populist thought-creators (state or non-state), often transition from matters of private code of conduct to public and penal code of conduct. This is as true for sectarian hate that festers within the borders of a state through dichotomous narratives of the "rightful" and the "pious" as opposed to the "immoral" and the "blasphemous", as it is for international wars (of conventional or unconventional sort) under the guise of "self-defense". In both such cases of exclusionary narratives—of sectarian hate and international wars—the notion of "self-defense" factors central. In the case of sectarian hate—or, for that matter, racial hate and other form of hate—the need to preserve the authenticity of religions and religious practices becomes framed as a matter of self-defense of sorts. In the case of international wars, particularly those conducted by states that seem perpetually involved in wars, notions of the need to protect their ways of being become framed as matters of self-defense, even if such notions of self-defense have very little to do with actually protecting and preserving the integrity of their state boundaries.

Richard Falk underscores the permeability of notions of morality and legality in his critique of the American "war on terror".[22] Falk's central argument, however, transcends his critique of the post-September 2001 (hereafter post-9/11) wars that America has fought under the guise of self-defense, as it outlines instead two universal tendencies of states, and, we can argue, non-state actors: first, the tendency to present actions (engaged in war) as legitimate (moral) when they do not otherwise qualify the parameters of legality (as set by international conventions and customs); and second, to argue that matters of legitimacy (morality) trump matters of legality at times.

Falk delivers a number of poignant arguments to this end: (1) notions of legality are often overridden by notions of legitimacy (morality) whenever there may be discrepancy between the two; (2) wherever the international legality of an action is missing or sketchy, notions of some universal morality and legitimacy are invoked; (3) the overlooking of notions of international legality in the interests of what is presented as legitimate (moral and thus imperative) is often linked directly to realist self-interests and national-interests. In other words, he argues, "the realities of geopolitics are such that powerful states often disregard the sovereignty of weaker states and also ignore binding obligations of international law".[23] Falk further points out:

> Advocates of harsh interrogation techniques after 9/11 in the United States pushed aside the constraints of the Geneva Convention and the anti-torture norm as commonly understood. Despite the reassurances from leaders that "torture" was reserved for exceptional circumstances associated with ticking-bomb scenarios and the avoidance of future 9/11 attacks, reliance on torture became widespread in various prisons under American military command.[24]

In other words, the *illegitimacy* (immorality) and *illegality* of torture became presented in legitimate (moral) terms, or, more accurately, in moral consequentialist terms: where the ends of larger self-defense (as in seeking to avoid another 9/11) were invoked to moralize the means (torture) towards that end. Falk understands the exceptionalism inherent in American hypocrisy—of violating international law while on the other hand justifying its wars in the name of the sanctity of international law—as based on the very nature of the notions of self-defense: namely, its subjectivity. However, Falk acknowledges that "there are exceptional circumstances that appear morally and politically to call for a suspension or evasion of normal legality".[25] But here again, he argues that this results in a dilemma that "can be expressed as one of a rigid insistence that no global understanding is justifiable if it appears contrary to international law and the opposite claim that global leadership tends to be beholden to a geopolitical logic that often supersedes the guidelines provided by law".[26]

The subjectivity that blurs the distinction between legality and legitimacy can also be seen, I argue, in the justifications of unconscionable acts committed by non-state actors. Examples include non-state actors of the likes of Islamic State (radical Islamic terrorist movement), Kahana Chai (radical Jewish terrorist group), Ku Klux Klan (American radical white supremacist group), and the myriad versions of contemporary neo-Nazi groups (in the United States and Europe). All such non-state actors justify their inhumanity and brutality in the name of self-defense of sorts, and therefore in the name of legality (defined in religious or secular terms), and thus in the name of morality (again, defined in religious or secular terms).

Perhaps the most controversial example of the merging of the notions of legitimacy (morality) and legality is found in Eichmann's own defense at his trial in Jerusalem in 1961. Eichmann, as a prominent Nazi-SS Kommandant in Auschwitz, argued that his actions of active complicity with the Nazi regime's extermination policy were, in fact, *morally imperative* precisely because they were legally imperative.[27] To put it simply, he argued that he was a moral person who sought to follow the categorical imperative of duty. And since his duty called upon him to facilitate the extermination of Jews and a myriad of other innocent human being (gypsies, political dissidents), these calls, he argues, were therefore legally and morally imperative. And that following his duty unquestionably and categorically thus relegated him to a morally upstanding citizen of the highest degree.[28] It is precisely such perverted logic that, in fact, normalized the violence and brutality of the Nazi regime in the eyes of its collaborators, supporters, and perpetrators.

Popularizing violence

The notion of the necessity of violence is fundamentally constructed through popularizing violence as the "will of the people". So while the narratives of violence are constructed with reference to a multi-pronged logic that includes both notions of morality and legality (as I have outlined previously), their necessity is constructed through presenting such violent actions as being for the good of the silent majority, the forgotten, the downtrodden. And the individual or group that spins inhumanity as popular representation becomes revered as the hero, the entity (individual or group) that came to the rescue of the forgotten: the savior that stopped at nothing to finally represent the forgotten majority, even if through harsh and unpopular policies.

Bernard Crick defines populism as "a style of politics which, if certainly not wholly new" breaks "from the manner of careful, reasoned argument".[29] We may understand this as a style of politics that rhetorically arouses fanaticism of the left or the right, as the case may be. It is also, of course, a style that "seeks to arouse a majority, or at least *what their leaders passionately believe is a majority*".[30] In fact, the construction of the notions of the "majority" is the very defining component of populist narratives. This is because it is such narratives, and the populist's rhetoric of *representing* this "majority", that are central to its appeal. Indeed, populism may be understood as a dynamic spearheaded by the populist (mobilizer or leader), under the guise of "authentic democratic representation"—of the constructed "majority"—that offers it an appeal. And when notions of the majority are constructed to represent only a particular racial, religious, or ethnic group, it is also this very dynamic of "selection" that lends populism its toxic nature. And it is this toxic nature that inevitably, and almost naturally, normalizes violence.

We may also understand populism with reference to Alexis de Tocqueville's notion of the "tyranny of the majority".[31] And as before, the notion of "majority" is both subjective and contingent to the popular base of the populist. Tocqueville describes this tyranny of the majority as "tyranny over the mind, not over the body".[32] This is a critical point here as it underscores the momentum and the gravitational pull of populist rhetoric, as a result of which the promotions of even unspeakable atrocities (of violence, human rights violations, monstrosity) are accepted wholesale. It is such blind faith that, Tocqueville argues, gives rise to the tyranny over the minds of the masses. In other words, the masses of the populist are not oppressed in the physical sense of those who live under authoritarian political systems, rather they are oppressed through their own desperate and banal desire to accept the narratives that suddenly give them importance and recognition. It is also within this context that we can understand, once again, Tocqueville's critique of American democracy as epitomized by a culture of mediocrity. Or, to put it in more sensational terms, "the greatest danger to democracy comes out of democracy".[33]

Critical to our understanding of the normalization of violence under the banner of "we the people"—or under the banner of the populist's rhetoric of "popular representation"—is the fact that the culture of mediocrity and the tyranny of the majority that it results in, as described by Tocqueville, is both based on and leads to the uncritical acceptance of any and all actions espoused by the populist as being truly good for the majority. This sheds instructive light on the dynamics of the current Trump administration in the United States, and the ability of this administration to engage in policies of unapologetic discrimination and inhumanity that were previously considered contrary to the very liberal nature of American democracy. And it is this dynamic that is thus responsible, I argue, for unconscionable policies such as separating children from their parents as part of a deportation policy to address illegal immigration, or banning Muslims from countries deemed as threats to the United States collectively and without discretion.[34] Much of the violence that has resulted from the fomenting of radical reactionary groups—whether that of the radical right (White Nationalists, Alt-Right, Neo-Nazis) or the radical left—as a result of Trump's policies have been, de facto, normalized as the growing pains of political transitions. It is also precisely in this way that the Trump administration has presented the inhumanities and violence of its policies, as necessary to challenge the despotism of the intellectual elite that is supposedly disconnected from the masses, and the despotism of illegal immigration and even international trade that are presented as encroaching on American sovereignty.[35] Ultimately, we may conclude, I argue, that when populists promote violence, populism moves from the realm of the *inclusionary* to the realm of the *exclusionary*. And it is at this point that populism becomes transformed into what I call "toxic populism".[36]

Dissemination of narratives: manufacturing consent

Noam Chomsky and Edward Herman's pivotal book, *Manufacturing Consent: The Political Economy of the Mass Media* (1988), is perhaps one of the most defining works of our time, and yet a work whose warnings are increasingly forgotten by our contemporaries.[37] Popularized as Noam Chomsky's notion of manufacturing consent, this book explains what I call the tyranny of the mass media in supporting and reinforcing its political friends in the higher echelons of the political system in the following ways: (1) framing violence and wars in ways that would be palatable to the audiences (the masses); (2) establishing and determining, on their own, what issues qualify as "real" security threats warranting their publicization; and (3) popularizing the idea of violence through presenting the policies of violence as catering to the demands of the people for accountability and defense, and as thus "representative" or "democratic".

In the case of the first point, Chomsky and Herman argue that the violence of wars is presented in palatable terms to its audiences by downplaying its most ugly and inhumane manifestations, while at the same time highlighting its positive outcomes, such as, for example, the resultant liberation of a people or the consequent protection of a people from worst fates. Consent for wars is thus manufactured through whitewashing its ugliness while highlighting its positive outcomes. In the case of the second point, Chomsky and Herman argue that it is the very ability of the media to selectively highlight certain issues, as reflective of their own vested interests, and to thus focus primarily on those issues that offer the media its monopoly in information dissemination. It must be noted here, however, that this monopoly has now been challenged through the onset of social media as a contending narrative-creator and disseminator of news. And the fact that social media—especially venues such as Twitter—can deliver a story to the audience while it is happening, in real time, is what has given social media not only the competitive edge against traditional media, but it has also therefore challenged the monopoly of traditional media. Consent is still being manufactured through social media, except now such consent is based on genuinely contradictory narratives and raw stories that, by virtue of their massive scale and their acute diversity, cannot be blamed for monopolizing narratives. And finally, to the third point above, Chomsky and Herman argue that traditional media has traditionally offered only part of a story in its efforts to manufacture consent for actions or wars that it deems will benefit its own economic interests and investment potentials.

While media—where traditional media or social media, in print or audiovisual forms—has typically been viewed as creating and dispensing narratives intended to shape the sensibilities of mass society, a silent but pivotal contender has typically been underestimated and ignored for its role in the manufacturing of consent for actions (particularly controversial actions). And this contender is none other than iconography. Iconography, of course, is both a sub-discipline within art history, as well as a phenomenon in itself. In the reminder of this section, I focus on iconography as a subtle but powerful tool for the manufacturing of consent.

Iconography

Roelof van Straten notes that a work of art, or an image, elicits a stock question: "Who is the artist?"[38] This is followed by other common questions: "What does the work of art depict?" and "What is the theme or subject of this work of art?"[39] Iconography, he notes, is that "field within art history that is exclusively concerned with answering this question".[40] But iconography is not only concerned with the obvious theme and subject of an image, it is also concerned with what van Straten refers to as "deeper meanings or content".[41] We may understand the meaning of "deeper meanings" with reference to the work of art historian Meyer Schapiro. In his book *Words and Pictures: On the Literal and the Symbolic in the Illustration of a Text*,[42] Schapiro makes a distinction between the "'literal' and the 'symbolic' meanings in both image and text".[43] The literal meaning of an image—a painting, photograph, sculpture, or political cartoon—is often obvious as it is the glaring component one notices at first sight. But the symbolic meaning requires contemplation, and, more importantly, *contextualization* of the image. Michel Foucault explains the importance of the contextualization of an image by arguing that an image has a life of its own, and indeed "acquires new dimensions of meaning in every new context that it encounters".[44] This means that the deeper meaning of an image is contingent upon two things: popular sensibilities of people in its original context, and the popular sensibilities of people in the context that it is being viewed, if other than its original context. Here, by "context" I mean the physical and temporal context of a place and people wherein the image was created, and the physical and temporal context of the people who come to view the image beyond its place of birth or creation. This means that whatever is symbolized in the image is never explicitly depicted or portrayed, as the meaning (symbolism) of the image rests in the eye of the beholder, or in the mind of the beholder.[45]

The distinction between literal and symbolic meanings is perhaps nowhere more relevant than in the iconic images of the Abu Ghraib scandal in 2003. In his book *Cloning Terror: The War of Images, 9/11 to the Present*, W.J.T. Mitchell focuses on the image of the hooded Iraqi torture victim, standing on a box with his arms raised downwards at a 60 degree angle from his torso, with electrodes attached to his fingers and genitals (the latter not visible in the image). He asks why that particular image became iconic, not only for the Abu Ghraib scandal but also for the broader American war on terror. Fundamentally, Mitchell explains the iconographic importance of the image by noting that both the image, and the particular psychological torture technique that it encompasses, were rumored to depict the "Jesus position".[46] In her testimony at a military tribunal in 2005, US Army Reservist Sabrina Harman—who was one of the six US military personnel indicted by the US Army for mistreating and torturing Iraqi prisoners at Abu Ghraib prison—said that she took pictures of the Iraqi torture victims because their stress positions "looked like Jesus Christ".[47]

Mitchell argues that it is not so much the fact that the Iraqi prisoner was *hooded* that is important—though being hooded offered anonymity to the torture victim, which, ironically, allowed for the image to take on a symbolic meaning—it is instead the position of the raising of the arms downwards at an angle that is significant. This is because the raising of the arms downwards at an angle offers a "Christological gesture"[48]: it suggests Christian iconography of either "Christ crucified",[49] or, more appropriately, Christ resurrected, since in the latter Christ has his arms raised downwards, as does the Iraqi torture victim.[50]

In order to understand and appreciate how the image of the Iraqi hooded man came to take on a Christological gesture and how, therefore, the image came to normalize violence in Abu Ghraib prison and in the larger war on terror, we must turn again to Meyer Shapiro's dichotomy of the literal and the symbolic meaning of an image, as well as Michel Foucault's context-contingent meaning of the image. Quite simply, then, while the literal meaning of the hooded man was torture of Iraqis at the hands of the American military in Iraq, the symbolic meaning revolved around the Christological gesture. Or, as Mitchell refers to it colloquially: "Jesus Comes to Abu Ghraib".[51] In its context-contingent meaning, while the hooded man in the "Jesus position" implicitly and symbolically resonated in the American context as a symbol of redemption of sorts—as Americans redeeming themselves through the war on terror, and as Iraqis redeeming themselves from their evil through being punished in the war on terror—it resonated explicitly in the Iraqi context as oppression and injustice at the hands of the Americans. But since the American war on terror has depended on the sentiments of the American public at large for its perpetuation, it is the symbolic and the American context-contingent meaning of the hooded man that becomes important. In other words, its Christological gesture comes to veil the atrocities committed at Abu Ghraib prison, and to thereby normalize violence committed in the name of the "war on terror".

In the case of *war* iconography, the intention of the image creators is always to *manufacture consent* for the war, either in the form of support for, or rejection of, the war. The left-wing pacifists are therefore likely to disseminate those visuals and images that *invoke* repulsion over how a war is being conducted. Whereas right-wing warmongers are likely to disseminate those visuals and images that *evoke* fear of the enemy as a way to manufacture consent in favor of war. Indeed, Mitchell argues that former President Bush's "war on terror" essentially became a "war of images" (of the aggressors versus the victims). And so while the American pro-war contingencies saw the images as confirmation of the necessity of war, the "enemy" saw the images as confirmation of their oppression at the hands of the Americans, thereby conformation of the need to violently resist the Americans.

Getty Images[52] provides an insightful visual commentary on the American "war on terror" with its 60 most iconic photographs from the war.[53] A mere cursory look at these photographs reveals an interesting narrative. The pictures are nestled in more or less the following order: a dead Taliban soldier; American soldiers preparing for their mission in Afghanistan; silhouette of American soldiers diligently saluting the American flag; an emotional, passionate embrace goodbye between a woman and a male American soldier; President Bush in his Oval Office, looking somber and determined; a distant silhouette of an individual falling out of the burning Twin Towers on 9/11; American soldiers engaging in emotional farewells with their spouses and their baby; local weapons-yielding Afghanis looking determined and angry; wounded American soldiers with bloody faces and innocent expressions; photo of the burning Twin tTwers; American soldiers busy interacting with local Afghani male adults; local Afghani children fraternizing with American soldiers, who, while uniformed and armed, have friendly face expressions; picture of Osama bin Laden with the caption "Justice Has Been Done", narrating the capture of bin Laden by American special forces; picture of the burning Twin Towers again; American soldiers eating with fellow comrades and with members of the local Afghani armed forces; picture of the burning towers, once again; and so on.

A quick glance at these photos reveals a one-sided story, that of the victims of 9/11 terrorism, but it doesn't reveal the other side of the story, that of the innocent civilians in the enemy's domain. In whitewashing the other side of the story, these photographs are an iconographic representation of the "good American", the victim, the brave, the soldier committed to duty and country. And as such, these pictures manufactured, and manufacture, consent for the more than two decades long "war on terror". But what these pictures do not reveal, by design—as such a revelation would do the opposite of manufacturing consent for the war—is the dark side of the war on terror: namely, the CIA's extraordinary renditions program, often involving mistaken identities and thus innocent individuals; torture for the ends of the war on terror, as in, though not limited to, the Abu Ghraib prison debacle in Iraq, and the alleged torture in Bagram Air Base (the largest US military base) in Afghanistan; Afghani and Iraqi civilian causalities; and abuses of power at the hands of the American military personnel, such as rape and disproportionate use of force.

Final reflections

It may seem curious that I distinguish narratives (manufacturing enemy) from the dissemination of narratives (manufacturing consent) in the analysis in this chapter. Surely, one might argue, the creation of narratives (manufacturing enemies) is inseparable from the dissemination of these narratives (manufacturing of consent). However, my reason to draw a distinction between the two is to emphasize the different stages *within* the process of violence: stage one is the creation of the narratives, while stage two is the dissemination of those narratives.

It may also seem curious that I distinguish between discourse and iconography as forms of narrative dissemination. It can be argued that iconography is a discourse of sorts, albeit one that is visual and symbolic, as opposed to verbal and explicit. But again, my intention in making this clear distinction between discourse and iconography is to highlight the two very different forms of narrative communication, and to further underscore the significance of iconography in the normalization of violence. I maintain that iconography, as a mode of communication and dissemination of narratives, is often overlooked and undervalued. Yet, it is perhaps the most immediate and automatic mode of narrative dissemination as it both does not require literacy and it can be observed, and its message comprehended, while the viewer is going about their daily lives, such as, for example, driving past billboards or walls of graffiti that deliver the message through a few quick seconds of a glance.

Beyond these two qualifications, I have argued in this chapter that from the narratives of the divinity of violence, to violence as "standard operating procedures", to delineating the necessity of violence as a means of popular representation, we see a common thread: that of the presentation of violence as necessary, ordinary, and unremarkable, intended to take the sting out of the monstrosity of violence and thus to normalize violence. Hannah Arendt's notion of the banality of evil sheds light on this phenomenon, which George Kateb describes as a situation where the wrongdoer does not recognize their violent and brutal actions as being wrong, morally or legally; this, notes Kateb, is in sharp contrast to the Shakespearean character Macbeth, who "owns", if you may, his evil nature and his evil deeds.

Committing evil is disturbing enough; committing evil and not knowing that you are committing evil is surely by far the worst of all horrors, for in such a situation, there are no limits to the atrocities that can be committed as the absence of conscience allows the unconscionable to take place, all in a matter of a day's work.

The manner in which Arendt's notion of the banality of evil is misunderstood, as meaning that the acts of violence and brutality are commonplace and therefore not notable, ironically describes the phenomenon itself: namely, the reframing of the violence one commits as being merely a standard operating procedure. The fact that both the manufacturing of enemies, and the manufacturing of mass consent to use violence against the enemies, relies upon rational and consequentialist logic showcases its synthetic, *a priori*, and contingent nature. The relative ease with which these narratives are synthesized further contributes to the normalization of violence, if only because the frameworks for these narratives, and the methods to dispense these narratives effectively and en masse, are already always there. In other words, the broad conceptual categories of the narratives of violence—moralizing, legalizing, popularizing—and the venues for their dissemination—media and discourse of sorts and iconography—are always ever readily present, as if they were a mathematical formula wherein all one needed to do is to punch in the specifics of a case in point.

I have also argued that the dogmatic and self-righteous nature of the notions of morality lend themselves to being fused into notions of legality. The logic is simple: if something is moral, it ought to be legal; and if something is legal, it ought to be moral. Such a two-fold logic, along with all its subjectivities, is then utilized by populist mobilizers to present their policies as not only moral and legal but as also therefore necessary for the integrity of a nation. Now suddenly, violent and brutal policies become normalized as the only policies truly representative of "we the people". That is, policies become viewed not in terms of their violent and brutal nature, but in terms of their "necessary" and representative nature. Prejudice, inhumanity, and violence of all sorts then get justified as the "growing pains" of an upstanding society concerned primarily with its security. For example, America's Trump administration justifies its exclusionary domestic and international policies as necessary redress to the despotism of the intellectual elite, illegal immigrants, and even foreign trade.

It is important to note that the normalization of violence through narrative creation is not a one-sided story. That is, the construction of the other as evil takes place simultaneously with the deconstruction of the evil that the self engages in. This further normalizes violence as it casts the self as purely and unequivocally a victim, while the other as purely and unequivocally the aggressor. The absurdity of this narrative is highlighted by Stathis Kalyvas who argues that in reality, the distinction between aggressors and victims is often—if not always—blurred. In other words, in situations of violence in reality, the self, and the other, is always both a victim and an aggressor. It is perhaps this nebulous nature of the dynamics of violence that further normalizes violence through blurring who is the real aggressor or the victim in acts of violence and inhumanity. After all, every evildoer has his own story that, at the very least, puts into question the action-reaction dynamic of violence. This works therefore to pacify the critique levied against the aggressors, which thereby, again, only serves to normalize their acts of violence and brutality.

A few critical points regarding the modes of narrative dissemination, and how they serve to normalize violence, are in order here. Noam Chomsky and Edward Herman's classic work on manufacturing consent offers insights into how violence and wars come to be normalized through the (traditional) media's selective reporting of atrocities committed, victims created, and outcomes generated. The argument is that the media spins the facts so that the self appears as righteous and the other as atrocious, the self as the victim and the other as the aggressor, and the self as generating outcomes of liberation and freedoms while the other as being hell-bent on destroying liberty and freedoms. Clearly, of course, the more fluid, "real-time" reporting of social media, such as Twitter, has now challenged the monopoly of traditional media. To be sure, social media reporting still seeks to manufacture consent in favor of the self and the cause that the self belongs to, but since anyone and everyone has access to this media outlet, the narratives disseminated are genuinely diverse and set into motion a play of narratives and counter-narratives.

Finally, iconography as mode of narrative dissemination is perhaps—at least to me—the most fascinating and insidious, both because its messages are variable and context-contingent, and because there is always a literal (explicit) and symbolic (implicit) meaning in its images. Here, works of Meyer Schapiro, Michel Foucault, and W.J.T. Mitchell are significant. The example that I focused on in this chapter, as inspired by Mitchell's analysis, is that of the now-iconic image of the hooded Iraqi torture victim, taken from the images that have come to narrate the Abu Ghraib prison scandal. This is a particularly important image as while it is, in its literal terms, an image of a compromised Iraqi prisoner under the American watch, in its symbolic terms, it yields two radically different meanings to different people in different contexts, both of which, ironically, serve to normalize violence but for two very different reasons. In the American, predominately Christian context, Mitchell argues that the image has a Christological significance, with the hooded prisoner's arms raised downwards as if reminiscent of the imagery of Christ resurrected. As such, Mitchell argues that the image exudes a symbolic reference to salvation which, he contends, serves to implicitly contribute to the narratives that we, the Americans, are doing good in the wars abroad, perhaps even offering salvation to the Iraqis from their violent ways of being. In this way, this image normalizes violence for those Americans that are not able to go past its Christian iconography. This image, however, has a very different literal and symbolic meaning for the Iraqis, or conceivably, for any other observer outside the Christian world, to whom the image is a symbolization of American tyranny, vulgarity, and monstrosity, against whom any violence is thus merely a recourse and therefore both moral and legal. And so here again we go back to the dynamics of the morality-legality-popularity formulae that normalizes violence universally.

Notes

1 The international standards of proportionality, as stated in the internationally accepted Just War Doctrine, can perhaps be best understood with reference to how natural law proponents understand this stipulation, namely: "anticipated overall evils of war must be less than overall good likely to be achieved". See Alex J. Bellamy's analysis of just war doctrine in his book, *Just Wars: From Cicero to Iraq* (Cambridge, UK: Polity Press, 2008), p. 127.
2 For Hannah Arendt's analysis of Stalin and Hitler's regimes, see *The Origins of Totalitarianism* (New York: A Harvest Book, 1976).
3 A 'Kommandant' was the title given to the chief commanding officer in the Nazi death camps.
4 See Hannah Arendt, *Eichmann in Jerusalem: A Report on the Banality of Evil*, introduction by Amos Elon (New York: Penguin Books, 2006).
5 Excerpts from Arendt's *Eichmann in Jerusalem* (1963), as quoted by Elisabeth Young-Bruehl in her book *Why Arendt Matters*, in her analysis of Arendt's reconstruction of Eichmann's conscience.
6 A passage from Arendt's *Eichmann in Jerusalem* (1963), as quoted by Elisabeth Young-Bruehl in her book *Why Arendt Matters*, pp. 3–4.
7 George Kateb, "Fiction as Poison", in *Thinking in Dark Times: Hannah Arendt on Ethics and Politics*, edited by Roger Berkowitz, Jeffrey Katz, and Thomas Keenan (New York: Fordham University Press, 2010), p. 31.
8 See George Kateb's analysis of Hannah Arendt in "Fiction as Poison", p. 30.
9 George Kateb's analysis of Hannah Arendt in "Fiction as Poison", p. 30. Emphasis added here and does not appear in the original text.
10 George Kateb's analysis of Hannah Arendt in "Fiction as Poison", p. 30; emphasis appears in Kateb's original text.
11 Salvador Giner, *Mass Society* (New York: Academic Press, Inc., 1976).
12 Giner, *Mass Society*, p. 76.
13 Giner, *Mass Society*, p. 78.
14 See Stanley Milgram, *Obedience to Authority*, foreword by Philip Zimbardo (New York: Harperperennial, 2009).
15 See Philip Zimbardo, *The Lucifer Effect: Understanding How Good People Turn Evil* (New York: Random House Trade Paperbacks, 2008).

16 David Frankfurter, "The Construction of Evil and the Violence of Purification", in *The Oxford Handbook of Religion and Violence*, edited by Mark Juergensmeyer, Margo Kitts, and Michael Jerryson (New York: Oxford University Press, 2013), pp. 521–532.
17 James Jones, "Religion and Violence from a Psychological Perspective", in *The Oxford Handbook of Religion and Violence*, edited by Mark Juergensmeyer, Margo Kitts, and Michael Jerryson (New York: Oxford University Press, 2013), pp. 393–396.
18 See Irm Haleem, *The Essence of Islamist Extremism: Recognition through Violence, Freedom through Death* (New York: Routledge, 2012).
19 See Anil Gupta's "Supplement on 'Experience'", in *Empiricism and Experience* (New York: Oxford University Press, 2006), pp. 223–236.
20 Epistemological distinctions drawn from Christine M. Korsgaard's analysis in "Introduction", in *Kant, Groundwork of the Metaphysics of Morals*, edited by Mary Gregor (Cambridge: Cambridge University Press, 1997).
21 For further clarifications and epistemological distinctions, see Korsgaard, "Introduction".
22 See Richard Falk, "Introduction: Legality and Legitimacy: Necessities and Problematics of Exceptionalism", in *Legality and Legitimacy in Global Affairs*, edited by Richard Falk, Mark Juergensmeyer, and Vesselin Popovski (New York: Oxford University Press, 2012), pp. 3–42.
23 Falk, "Introduction: Legality and Legitimacy", p. 4.
24 Falk, "Introduction: Legality and Legitimacy", p. 5.
25 Falk, "Introduction: Legality and Legitimacy", p. 4.
26 Falk, "Introduction: Legality and Legitimacy", p. 6.
27 See Arendt, *Eichmann in Jerusalem*.
28 See Hannah Arendt's critical and ironic analysis of Eichmann's narratives in his own defense in *Eichmann in Jerusalem*.
29 Bernard Crick, *Democracy: A Very Short Introduction* (New York: Oxford University Press, 2002), p. 77.
30 Crick, *Democracy*, p. 77. Emphasis is added here and does not appear in the original text.
31 See Alexis de Tocqueville, *Democracy in America: And Two Essays on America*, translated by Gerald Bevan, with an Introduction and Notes by Isaac Kramnick (New York: Penguin Books, 2003).
32 See Harvey C. Mansfield's analysis of Tocqueville in *Tocqueville: A Very Short Introduction* (New York: Oxford University Press, 2010), p. 58.
33 See Mansfield's analysis of Tocqueville in *Tocqueville*, p. 57.
34 The analysis of the politics involved in the American designation of 'threat countries' is beyond the scope of this chapter. It may suffice here to simply acknowledge that politics leads to contradictory conclusions.
35 The issue of illegal immigration is indeed both controversial and complicated as, I argue, it is true by virtue of customary international law that illegal immigration does indeed violate the sovereignty of the host state. And so some part of the Trump administration's rhetoric—as characteristic of any populist leader's rhetoric—is based on legitimate facts of sovereignty and incursions to sovereignty. A detailed and nuanced analysis of this topic, however, is beyond the scope of this chapter.
36 I analyze this notion in more detail elsewhere; however, a detailed analysis of what I call 'toxic populism' is beyond the scope of this chapter.

37 See Edward Herman and Noam Chomsky, *Manufacturing Consent: The Political Economy of the Mass Media* (New York: Pantheon Books, 1988).
38 Roelof van Straten, *An Introduction to Iconography* (New York: Taylor & Francis Group, 2000), p. 3.
39 van Straten, *An Introduction to Iconography*, p. 3.
40 van Straten, *An Introduction to Iconography*, p. 3.
41 van Straten, *An Introduction to Iconography*, p. 3.
42 Meyer Schapiro, *Words and Pictures: On the Literal and the Symbolic in the Illustration of a Text* (Berlin: Mouton De Gruyter, 1973).
43 See William John Thomas Mitchell's analysis of Meyer Schapiro's contribution to iconography in W.J.T. Mitchell, *Cloning Terror: The War of Images, 9/11 to the Present* (Chicago: The Chicago University Press, 2011), p. 144.
44 See W.J.T. Mitchell's analysis of Michel Foucault's contribution to iconography in Mitchell, *Cloning Terror*, p. 149.
45 See Roelof van Straten's analysis of symbols and symbolic representation of images in *An Introduction to Iconography*, p. 45.
46 Mitchell, *Cloning Terror*, p. 141.
47 See Mitchell's narration of Sabrina Harman's testimony in Mitchell, *Cloning Terror*, p. 141.
48 Mitchell, *Cloning Terror*, p. 147.
49 See references to Christ crucified in Mitchell, *Cloning Terror*, pp. 144, 150.
50 Mitchell, *Cloning Terror*, p. 150.
51 This is part of a title of Mitchell's chapter, "State of the Union, or Jesus Comes to Abu Ghraib", in *Cloning Terror: The War of Images, 9/11 to the Present* (Chicago: The Chicago University Press, 2011).
52 Wikipedia describes Getty Images, Inc. as a "visual media company"—headquartered in Seattle, Washington, United States—with the aim of distributing images for creative professionals, the media, and the corporate sectors. The relevance of Getty Images here, I argue, is how these images create and contribute to iconography.
53 See Getty Images, "60 Top War on Terror Pictures", www.gettyimages.com/photos/war-on-terror?sort=mostpopular&mediatype=photography&phrase=war%20on%20terror&license=rf,rm&page=1&recency=anydate&suppressfamilycorrection=true

2 Moralizing militarism through educational curriculum in Japan

Naoko Kumada

The Moritomo Gakuen scandal that recently embroiled the Abe administration brought to popular attention a 128-year-old document called the Imperial Rescript of Education (*kyōiku chokugo* 教育勅語) (1890). It is a "sacred teaching"[1] on the principles of education the Meiji Emperor gave to the people—then called "subjects (*shinmin* 臣民)", not "citizens"—and taught at elementary schools in pre-war Japan, when Japan was a Shinto state. From around the Meiji Restoration (1868) until the end of World War II (1945), Japan was governed through a *religio*-political system based on a newly invented State Shintoism.[2] The Imperial Rescript of Education, designed to systematically inculcate the people with an Emperor system ideology,[3] served as practically a "sacred scripture"[4] for the newly constructed State Shinto, and as the foundation of school education.[5] Together with the Imperial Rescript to Soldiers and Sailors (*gunjin chokuyu* 軍人勅諭) (1882), which included the notorious clause "the obligation is heavier than the mountains but death is lighter than a feather"[6] that soldiers needed to memorize and recite, it formed the core of moral education in State Shinto. Both these Rescripts served to nurture the Emperor's subjects into holding as their highest value the sacrifice of their lives for the Emperor. State Shinto turned increasingly militaristic, as Japan became imperialist as it fought the Sino-Japanese War (1894–95) and the Russo-Japanese War (1904–05),[7] and developed militaristic values glorifying suicide attacks[8] by the time Japan fought World War II. Japanese militarism during World War II unleashed unprecedented wartime violence that created 20 million victims in Asia.[9] Japan adopted a pacifist Constitution after it lost the war. The Japanese National Diet, the national legislature, then passed a resolution eliminating and invalidating both the Imperial Rescript of Education and the Imperial Rescript to Soldiers and Sailors in 1948, as they were deemed to be incompatible with the new Constitution which now based itself on human rights and popular sovereignty.

Today, the Abe administration draws on the same militant ideology of State Shintoism that anchored the militarism of pre-war Japan. In this chapter, I argue that the revival of moral education in Japan today must be critically examined in the historical context of Shinto nationalism and its consequent ultra-nationalist outcomes. We are observing the resurgence of religious nationalism of a peculiarly total character. The chapter focuses on the religio-political system and ideology that produced wartime violence, rather than on violence itself. I will explore the characteristics of State Shinto ideology and Shinto nationalism and the ways in which they moralized, indeed sacralized, state violence,[10] in order to understand how pre-war ideology and nationalism are being revived and what their revival means to us today. In so doing, I will show that the Japanese case is significant in that the Shinto state not only moralized militarism and violence, but was morality itself.

The Imperial Rescript of Education and Shinto militarism

The Moritomo scandal revealed that the kindergarten run by Moritomo Gakuen had been making the children in its care recite the Imperial Rescript of Education. Before the end of World War II, the 315-character document had been recited at elementary schools throughout Japan by children who memorized it by heart. Although the document includes some traditional moral teachings drawing on Confucianism (e.g., on the proper conduct of relationships with parents, spouse, and siblings), its core function is to declare an education directly linked with State Shinto and based on religious values:[11] the sacred bond between the Emperor and his subjects, its divine origin, the sacred obligation of the subjects, the worship of Amaterasu (a Shinto Sun Goddess from whom the line of emperors are said to have descended), reverence for the Imperial ancestors, and veneration for the Emperor.[12] Furthermore, it orders the subjects to patriotically serve the "public" (公) in times of emergency, requiring them to sacrifice everything for the sacred rule of the Emperor in times of crisis such as war.[13]

Videos posted on YouTube show Moritomo kindergarteners reciting the Imperial Rescript of Education by heart, cheering Prime Minister Shinzō Abe for passing the Security Bills, and thanking him for protecting Japan.[14] The issue drew wide public attention, because Akie Abe, the Prime Minister's wife, praised the school's patriotic education and became its honorary principal.[15] The media, the education sector,[16] and the public expressed criticism and concern that the Imperial Rescript and the patriotic moral values based on State Shinto ideology could be re-introduced into the Japanese education system.

Many conservatives, among politicians and the public, however, have strongly supported the Imperial Rescript. The movement to re-introduce and promote patriotic moral education, including using the Imperial Rescript of Education in schools, has been resurgent. The Abe administration has pushed forward educational reform, and Japan officially re-introduced moral education in the school curriculum in 2018 in elementary schools and in 2019 in junior high schools.

Simultaneously, the Abe administration has moved to re-establish the Japanese military. In 2015, it passed new security bills allowing the use of collective self-defense and expanding the role of the Self-Defense Force. The administration has been increasing the defense budget and building up weapons, claiming they are adjustments to what it calls "the changing external environment", namely the threat of North Korea and the rise of China.[17] The administration has also been pushing constitutional reform to amend Article 9 and ultimately replace *in toto* the post-war pacifist Constitution with a revisionist constitution (*jishu kenpō* 自主憲法).[18] *Jishu kenpō* means a "self-authored" constitution, as opposed to the pacifist constitution that its proponents view as having been imposed on Japan after it lost the war. Given their open appeals to the ideology of pre-war Japan, these simultaneous "reforms" pave the way for the return of that era's militarism.

At the core of State Shinto was a political theology that identified Japan as *kokutai* (国体 national polity), a divine polity with the Emperor, a living god who embodies absolute value, at the center. State Shinto reached its peak between 1931 (marked by the Manchurian Incident when the Japanese military invaded northeastern China) and the end of World War II, a period Japanese scholars of religion call the "Fascist period".[19] Japanese militarism during this period developed a political theology that narrated Japan as a theocratic nation entrusted with the mission of extending a divine emperor's influence to the "eight corners of the world" (*hakkō ichiu* 八紘一宇).[20] In the typology of Fascism, the Japanese case is significant in that the state/emperor not only moralized militarism and violence, but *was morality itself*: Japan became "the True, the Good, and the Beautiful".[21] There was no standpoint above the divine state against which its actions could be judged, especially if these were executed by a military viewed in this vision as the "thigh and elbow"[22] of the nation-body of the Emperor. Thus the war the Empire of Japan fought was a "holy war".[23]

The Imperial Rescript of Education was the kernel of an education system that indoctrinated an entire population in this view. It was thus crucial for the formation of Shinto nationalism. European nationalism developed in nation-states with a *separation* of civil and religious authority. In contrast, the Meiji oligarchs developed Japanese nationalism by constructing a Shinto theocracy that combined Japan's *previously separate* civil and religious powers in the person of an Emperor worshipped as a living god. Joined with militarism, this made for an especially extreme and total form of nationalism. It mobilized individuals within a tightly nested structure of loyalties to "family", "province", and "state". The Abe administration has reverted to this highly loaded pre-war vocabulary in calling for the nurturing of love for the family, the provinces, and the nation in the new moral education curriculum that his government has been implementing. In this, too, the administration is reviving a pillar concept of pre-war nationalism.

Japan as "the True, the Good, and the Beautiful"

Though Japanese public response commenting on the YouTube videos of the Moritomo kindergarteners varies, many express support for the kindergarteners reciting the Imperial Rescript of Education. They claim that it is normal in other countries, like the US, to give patriotic education to schoolchildren.[24] Others express concern for the re-introduction of patriotic moral education in the school curriculum.

The general Japanese public today have little interest in and knowledge about the Imperial Rescript of Education or State Shinto, for many reasons: in pre-war Japan, people did not have the freedom to criticize, or even conduct an objective study of, State Shinto;[25] State Shinto has become harder to recognize, though it has survived in post-war Japan.[26]

The most notorious Japanese wartime violence took place during the Fascist period (1931–45). The root of the problem goes back a long way, however, to the beginning of the Meiji period, when the Meiji oligarchs began to create a theocratic Shinto state using the Emperor's spiritual authority to unite Japan.

That in respect of religion, Japanese nationalism developed in the opposite direction, so to speak, from European nationalism,[27] is important to understanding how it held such power over individuals. The conventional understanding of nationalism, reflecting the European experience, describes it as having proceeded hand in hand with secularization. Europe's absolute monarchies emerged in the post-Reformation separation of church from state, with dynastic monarchies monopolizing a newly defined secular domain. European nations underwent modernization and standardization (such as teaching standardized vernacular languages in standardized schools throughout the nation), and nationalism developed as populations began to imagine themselves as belonging to these new nations.[28]

In contrast, Japanese nationalism started as a deliberate and directed project from above, led by the new leaders of the Meiji government.[29] Facing Japan's forced opening to western trade under the guns of Commodore Perry's black ships, and attempting to avoid the subjugation they saw inflicted on neighboring countries, particularly on a once-powerful China, the Meiji oligarchs understood the role that a new ideology was needed in reconstructing Japan as a nation-state able to repel the west. The slogan, "Revere the Emperor and expel the barbarians" (*sonnō jōi* 尊王攘夷) spread through Japan. To implement Emperor veneration to unite the people, Meiji Japan adopted a theocracy based on the unity of religion with state, ritual with politics (*saisē icchi* 祭政一致). Accordingly, the Meiji oligarchs reorganized the previously diverse, pluralistic, and heterogenous Japanese society into a unified hierarchical one, with the newly created absolute monarch, indeed a god-Emperor at the summit.[30]

The oligarchs identified the Emperor with the sovereign, and centralized all forms of power—political, religious and moral, civil, and military—under him in order to build a strong sovereign nation-state. The Meiji oligarchs unified the political power of the Shogun and other feudal lords under the authority of the Emperor.[31] They also unified religious and moral power in his divinized person. The Emperor, whose religious authority derives from his performance of nation-wide agricultural rituals for harvest of rice,[32] was elevated into something like the God of monotheism, an onto-theological notion that would previously have been incomprehensible to a people whose religious world had until then been "secular"[33] (decentralized, or non-hierarchical and multiple, rather than being hierarchical and binary[34]). Local Shinto practices and shrines that had existed as heterogenous folk religion throughout Japan were now hierarchicalized and systematized and coded, with, at the top, the Ise Shrine, the seat of Amaterasu, the Sun Goddess, original ancestress of the Imperial line.[35] Under State Shinto, Shinto shrines became state organizations, while it subordinated Buddhism, Christianity, and various, often recalcitrant, Shinto sects (*kyōha shinto* 教派神道).[36] The Meiji government reinvented the Emperor as the father of all the Japanese people, thus promoting the idea of Japan as a family-state.[37] In addition, the Meiji government gave the Emperor the modern European role of a commander-in-chief of the military.[38]

State Shinto allowed other religions, such as Christianity, Buddhism, and various Shinto sects (*kyōha Shinto*) to enjoy the freedom of religion, but only within their subordinate position. The logic that State Shinto governed the "public" realm of State "ritual" (祭、祭祀) and morality (道徳), whereas other religions governed the "private" realm, justified the coexistence of saisē icchi (unity of ritual and politics/state) and *sēkyō bunri* (政教分離 translated as separation of state and religion or freedom of religion).[39] The Meiji Constitution (the Constitution of the Empire of Japan, 1889)[40] and the Imperial Rescript of Education served to further institutionalize State Shinto.[41]

Although the process was explained as "restoring" imperial rule, it was actually a new invention, implemented at the cost of destroying the decentralized, pluralistic, and heterogeneous characteristics of Japanese society,[42] and giving the Emperor power none of his ancestors ever had. The Meiji oligarchs thus constructed a Shinto theocracy that *collapsed* Japan's previously separate civil and religious powers in the person of a deified Emperor: the very reverse of secularization in the formation of the nation-states.

Thus, Japanese "ultra-nationalism" was not merely quantitatively "stronger" than European nationalism. It was *qualitatively* different in its "spiritual motive power" to "expand abroad and oppress at home", in the words of Masao Maruyama in his influential work on Japanese ultra-nationalism.[43] The separation of religion and state led modern European nation-states to leave matters of internal values such as truth and morality to the church, while the state built its sovereignty on formal legal structures.[44] Absolute monarchs, who previously stood on the doctrine of the Divine Right of Kings for "internal" or religious claims over their subjects, now called on external, formal, and objective bases for maintaining public order. Japan, however, never observed such limits between private and public domains in its formation of a modern state. No force like the church that claimed to rule an internal or countervailing realm existed. The Japanese government in the Meiji period sought the role Christian doctrine played in the matters of truth and morality in the kokutai doctrine.[45] Japanese nationalism thus exerted its claims over its subjects as the actual "internal" value, at once religious and civil, public and private, the fountain of "the True, the Good, and the Beautiful".[46] The Emperor, the personification of the newly absolute state, became simultaneously the font of religious, moral, and political power and the source of internal moral value. The Imperial Rescript of Education was issued in a context in which the Japanese state was a moral entity that had monopoly to determine values.[47] Unlike in Europe, where religion and morality devolved into a private realm that was in principle inviolate by the state, the Meiji state's State Shinto created a public realm centered on the civil and political cult of the Emperor from which no individual could escape, against which no value could lay contradictory claims. This was the basis of Japanese ultra-nationalism.

The Meiji government adopted western systems, knowledge, and technology for modernizing Japan, while it maintained the newly created Japanese ways of doing things as much as possible.[48] The state education system that the government newly adopted from the west became an efficient means for spreading Shinto nationalism. The Imperial Rescript of Education and Emperor veneration rituals were crucial in this process. Standardized Emperor veneration ceremonies, citing the Imperial Rescript of Education, began to be performed at schools on special days, such as Empire Day (February 11, commemorating the founding of the nation when the first Emperor Jinmu 神武天皇 was enthroned) and the Emperor's birthday. The Emperor and the Empress's portraits and copies of the Imperial Rescript of Education, as well as the place they were kept, began to be treated as sacred, and as time passed, as something one must protect even in exchange for life in the case of fire.[49]

State Shinto in fact had originated as a supposedly civil, non-religious innovation of the state for the inculcation of unity and obedience. With its development, however, Shinto nationalism spread and took root in Japanese society, where its core ideas emerged in new religious movements animating State Shinto "from below".[50] Such religious nationalist movements from below became a powerful and destructive force, eventually destroying Taisho democracy that had begun to flourish in the early 20th century, and escalating political violence. As riots and popular movements became common, the notorious Maintenance of the Public Order Act (治安維持法) was established in 1925, foreshadowing the "totalitarian system" of "all-out mutual surveillance".[51] The Act prohibited participation in any association that denied the Emperor-centered national polity (*kokutai*) or private ownership. The Act had a chilling effect on civil freedom, as it "was used not only against communism and socialism, but also broadly against new religions, Christianity, and various liberal movements".[52] The Great Depression hit Japan very hard in 1929, triggering the intensification of "militarism" and "totalitarianism", and bringing on so-called Showa Fascism.[53]

By the 1930s, the divinity of the Emperor came to be emphasized (before that the Emperor was considered more as a monarch), and became an object of worship for whom the people were willing to sacrifice their lives.[54] Ironically, the democratic trend that allowed the participation of the people from below, who had by then become the most enthusiastic adherents to State Shinto, led to a Fascist takeover. It had by then become "too difficult to contain the movement from below", the movement that attempted to "overturn the existing order by upholding" the State Shinto ideas such as the Imperial Way (*kōdō* 皇道), an Emperor-centered totalitarian idea that Shinto nationalists and right-wing young army officers espoused.[55]

These religious nationalist "movements from below" became interlinked with Showa Fascism, in which the people supported "ultra-nationalist" "terrorists".[56] Under Showa Fascism, the thought and speech control by the State intensified, and the people were conscripted.[57] The February 26 Incident (an abortive coup in 1936 caused by young army officers who led a radicalized Fascist movement espousing the Imperial Way and seeking reform towards a theocratic state directly ruled by the Emperor)[58] took place in 1936, increasing the military interference in the cabinet; the National General Mobilization Act (国家総動員法, allowing the State wartime mobilization of human and material resources) was issued in 1938; the triple alliance treaty was signed by Japan, Nazi Germany, and Fascist Italy, and the Imperial Rule Assistance Association (大政翼賛会 aimed at creating a totalitarian one-party state) was founded in 1940; and, finally, Japan entered the Pacific War in 1941.[59] As the war progressed and the situation became increasingly difficult for Japan, the Imperial Army and Navy adopted suicide attacks by young *kamikaze* (神風 God's Wind) pilots and *kaiten* (回天 return to heaven) underwater "human torpedoes", many of whom were practically forced to "volunteer" for the suicide missions.[60]

Love for the family, the provinces, and the nation

Maruyama describes that the idea of the family and the provinces (or native place, *kyōdo* 郷土) is a distinct feature of Japanese nationalist and Fascist ideology.[61] The state is often taken to be an extension of the family, the family and the provinces are taken to be the basic unit of social coherence, and patriotism manifests as love for the provinces (*kyōdo*). In this ideology, the individual submerges into the family and the provinces, and eventually the nation.[62]

Intertwined with Shinto nationalist movements, Fascism and totalitarianism developed over a long period, their roots going back to the founding of the centralized Shinto state after the Meiji Restoration.[63] Japanese Fascism, however, was most conspicuous between the early 1930s and the end of the war (1945). Japanese Fascism of this period is often referred to as "*Showa fashizumu*" (昭和ファシズム, Showa Fascism)[64] or "*fassho jidai*" (ファッショ時代, Fascist period, "fassho" taken from the Italian *fascio*).[65]

Japanese Fascism shares many characteristics with Italian and German Fascism: opposition to "individualistic liberalism" and "parliamentary politics", preference for "foreign expansion", glorification of "military build-up and war", focus on "racial myths and national essence", "rejection of class warfare based on totalitarianism, and the struggle against Marxism".[66] It, however, has its own distinct features.

First is the "family-system tendency", in which "the family system is extolled as the fundamental principle of the State structure".[67] The State structure was "considered an extension of the family". The Imperial House in the center was considered to be the head family of the branch families of the people. The idea of a family-state based on the virtues of loyalty and filial piety had in fact been the official ideology from the Meiji era. It, however, became more conspicuous with the later development of the Fascist movement that emphasized the Emperor-centered 'national polity' (*kokutai*) as a political slogan.[68]

Second is the high priority of the provincial (*kyōdo*) and the agrarian, in which the idea of provincial agrarianism appears in opposition to, and as a counterbalance against, the absolute state centered on the Emperor.[69] It is because the Fascist movement developed initially from the tension between the poor provinces and the powerful state. In the early 20th century, the economic gap widened between the rural poor, many who were farmers struggling to have food on the table, and the more affluent city dwellers, in cities like Tokyo that benefited from capitalism and urbanization with links to overseas cities like London. The rural areas severely suffered when the Great Depression hit Japan, exacerbating their already impoverished lives and escalating radicalized Fascist movements. Right-wing terrorist attacks, that included assassinations of prominent politicians and business leaders, occurred frequently after 1931.[70]

The extreme poverty in rural areas created an avenue for the army to interfere in politics. Many young army officers who radicalized were from the rural areas, who understood and sympathized with the plight of the young soldiers from those areas.[71] Rural farmers had been the mainstay of the Japanese military. They were known for their quality, and served as model soldiers of the Emperor's Army.[72] Many of them questioned why they needed to sacrifice their lives for the powerful nation, leaving behind their impoverished family who depended on them. Rural areas had also served as the foundation of the Japanese family-system.[73] The severe hardships of these soldiers and their families' lives became an issue that the central government could not ignore.[74]

The social and economic divide between the provinces and the state meant that the soldiers and the people were patriotic toward their own provinces, but not necessarily nationalistic toward the nation-state.[75] The Fascist movement in Japan was shaped by such tension between the state and the provinces, in which the latter was given high priority. After the February 26 Incident (1936), the military eventually took over the Fascist movement which had been led by the people from the bottom. Japanese Fascist and nationalist ideology thus tend to conceptualize Japan by positioning the provinces, not the state, at the center, while it simultaneously emphasizes the Emperor-centered absolute state power.[76]

The Shinto state, the absolute divine polity with the Emperor at the center, was abolished when Japan surrendered to the Allied nations accepting the terms of the Potsdam Declaration, ending the war in August 1945. The Allied nations subsequently placed Japan under occupation. The Potsdam Declaration required that "a new order" be established in Japan by driving out "militarism" and destroying "Japan's war-making power", removing "all obstacles to the revival and strengthening of democratic tendencies", and establishing "freedom of religion" and "respect for the fundamental human rights". The General Headquarters of the Allied nations also issued the Shinto Directive (*Shinto shirē* 神道指令) in 1945, in order to separate religion from state and abolish State Shinto, which they considered to have supported Japan's militarism and nationalism that led Japan to war.[77]

In 1946, the year the new Peace Constitution was promulgated, the Ministry of Education issued an official notification stating that the Imperial Rescript of Education should not be "the only source of education in Japan", nor be read in schools nor its copies be treated as an object of worship.[78] The Basic Act on Education, implementing the principles of the post-war Constitution, was established in 1947.[79] Concerned that such administrative measure was insufficient, the Japanese Diet further passed a resolution in 1948, eliminating and invalidating the Imperial Rescript of Education as being incompatible with the new Constitution's principles of human rights and popular sovereignty, and questionable from the perspective of international credibility.[80] In particular, the common understanding was that the requirement to serve the sacred rule of the Emperor violated popular sovereignty.[81] The resolution stated that the Imperial Rescript of Education was still being "misunderstood as though it maintains its characteristic as the guiding principle of national morality", and that the fact that it is based on "the view of a mythical national polity" violates basic human rights.[82] Such multiple steps were necessary to invalidate it, as the teaching had so deeply inculcated the people.

The conservative groups in Japanese society, however, have been dissatisfied that the Allied forces denied the Imperial Rescript of Education. They have considered the new Constitution and the 1947 Basic Act on Education as the symbol of the system left behind by the Allied occupation, and have been pursuing movements for constitutional and educational reforms.[83] One such group is a faction of the Liberal Democratic Party (LDP) politicians following former Prime Minister Nobusuke Kishi, current Prime Minister Shinzō Abe's grandfather.[84] Others include Shinto nationalist groups such as Nippon Kaigi (日本会議 Japan Conference), which wants to restore the Emperor-centered national polity by replacing *in toto* the post-war Constitution.[85]

The movement to re evaluate the Imperial Rescript of Education has accelerated in the 21st century, particularly under the Abe administration.[86] Without having to go so far as to re-introduce the Imperial Rescript of Education itself in the moral education curriculum as in pre-war Japan, or to amend the post-war Constitution, attempts to re-introduce nationalistic moral concepts drawing on pre-war ideology into Japanese society are being made through legislative and policy measures.

In 2006, the first Abe administration amended the 1947 Basic Act on Education to include nurturing "moral sense" and "the attitude of love" for "our country and the provinces (*waga kuni to kyōdo*)".[87] Moritomo Gakuen explains that the kindergarten introduced the recitation of the Imperial Rescript of Education based on the amendment, to fulfil the new goal of "nurturing the attitude of love for our country and the provinces" set by the Abe administration.[88] The former Chief Justice of the Supreme Court, Tōru Miyoshi, who was the former President of Nippon Kaigi, stated Nippon Kaigi's goal in 2007: "We should first amend the Basic Act on Education, restore the population's consciousness, and then attempt to amend the

Constitution".[89] Nurturing love for "the family" and "love for our country and the provinces (waga kuni to kyōdo)" were introduced in the teaching guidelines for the new moral education curriculum published by the Ministry of Education, Culture, Sports, Science and Technology in 2008.[90]

In 2017, the Third Abe Cabinet made a decision that the use of the Imperial Rescript of Education as a teaching material, in ways that do not violate the Constitution or the Basic Act on Education, is not denied.[91] The Fourth Abe Cabinet officially re-introduced moral education in the school curriculum in 2018 in elementary schools and in 2019 in junior high schools.[92]

Pre-war Japanese Fascist and ultra-nationalist ideology centering around the patriotic idea of Japan as an extension of the family and the provinces is being re-introduced into not only moral education in schools, but also the draft of a new constitution the LDP published in 2012. The LDP draft constitution obliges the people to respect the family and to defend the "country and the provinces (*kuni to kyōdo*)".[93] Furthermore, the 2013 National Security Strategy, issued as a Cabinet decision, states that nurturing "love for our country and the provinces (waga kuni to kyōdo)" is needed for strengthening the social foundation supporting national security.[94] These examples show that nurturing love for the family, the provinces, and the country, in other words nurturing the Japanese conceptualization of nationalism taken from pre-war ideology by means of moral education in the school curriculum, is an orchestrated effort linked to national defense and security policies, and to the ultimate revisionist goal of re-establishing a self-authored constitution aimed at restoring the pre-war national polity.

Final reflections

On the question of normalization of violence, I have shown that Japanese Fascism is significant in that the Shinto state not only moralized militarism and violence, but was morality itself: Japan was the True, the Good, and the Beautiful. I have also shown that pre-war Japanese Fascist and ultra-nationalist ideology tends to manifest as the love for the family, the provinces, and the country.

The exhibition hall in the Yasukuni Shrine displays the Imperial Rescript of Education and the Imperial Rescript to Soldiers and Sailors.[95] Seventy-three years from the end of World War II, how might the way moral education is taught in the classroom shape Japan's future nationalism? Although it may be unlikely that Japan will recover its pre-war imperial might or overarching kokutai ideology, Japanese pre-war nationalism will continue to shape Japan's future nationalism. As Maruyama wrote in 1951:

> There can be no complete break in history. Thus it is unthinkable that Japan's future nationalism will develop without having any connection

> with its previous form. Japan's future nationalism, whether it emerges as a reaction against the past, as a compromise with its heritage, or as a revival of the pre-war form, cannot escape being branded by its own past. How the conditions in the world, or at the very least in the Far-East, will look will depend considerably on which of these forms it assumes.[96]

There has always been a built-in tendency for Japan to revert to totalitarianism, because of the way Japan built itself as a theocratic nation-state after the Meiji Restoration.[97] The post-war regime represented by the Peace Constitution and legislations such as the Basic Act on Education (1947), largely implemented by the Allied forces but also supported by many Japanese, have prevented the return to the ultra-nationalist, totalitarian, and militarist state. Perhaps the first 70 years of post-war Japanese nationalism manifested more as a reaction against the pre-war past. The resurgence of Shinto nationalism today indicates a shift in Japanese nationalism. A new form of nationalism has begun to emerge.[98]

The Shinto state was morality itself in pre-war Japan, and moral education, particularly the Imperial Rescript of Education, inculcated Japanese children to patriotically serve the sacred rule of the Emperor by serving in times of "crisis" such as war. The Abe administration calls the situation Japan is facing today (the shrinking population, the threat of North Korea) a "national crisis", invoking the "national crisis" faced by the leaders of the Meiji Restoration.[99] While the government moves constitutional reforms to pave the way for the re-arming of Japan, educational reforms are drawing once more on the ideology of wartime Japan. We have yet to see how 21st-century Japanese nationalism will manifest. Will it be a reaction against—this time—70 years of post-war pacifism, and a revival of the pre-war nationalism? Or a compromise between the pre-war and post-war nationalisms? How moral education will be taught to schoolchildren in 21st-century Japan will be relevant to this question. What form 21st-century Japanese nationalism will assume will likely shape how the conditions in the world, or at least the Far East, will look.

Notes

1 Susumu Shimazono, *Kokka Shintō to Nihonjin* (Tōkyō: Iwanami Shoten, 2010), i.
2 Shigeyoshi Murakami, *Kokka Shintō* (Tōkyō: Iwanami Shoten, 1970); Shimazono, *Kokka Shintō to Nihonjin*. There is ongoing debate on the usefulness of the term "State Shinto" in the study of Japanese religion (Hardacre 2017). The Constitution does not of course name Shintoism as the religion of state. Rather it presupposes a newly state-constructed, reinvented "Shintoism" as a

meta-discourse, a theo-political discourse of state, above "religion". Shintoism was elevated by its being deemed *not* a religion. It was thereby universal and public relative to now particularized and privatized "religions" such as Buddhism and Christianity (on how the newly imported term "religion" was used in Meiji state formation, see Josephson's important *The Invention of Religion in Japan*, 2012). The Meiji state-building project called for the unity of ritual and politics (*saisē icchi*) around a sacred national polity (*kokutai*) centered on Emperor veneration. The Constitution was promulgated with high Shinto ritual and it begins with an oath (Imperial Oath at the Sanctuary of the Imperial Palace) reciting the Shinto creation story as the founding mythology of state. It defines the state as *shinkenteki kokutai*, a theocratic polity whose sovereignty is transmitted in direct and unbroken succession from Amaterasu, the goddess of the Sun. It announces an eternal polity founded in a god-emperor whose authority is indivisibly religious and secular. It is in this context that I refer to "State Shintoism" and describe Meiji state formation as a theo-political project. For further detail, see Naoko Kumada, "Theocracy vs Constitutionalism in Japan", *RSIS Working Paper*, no. 310 (May 2, 2018), upon which this chapter builds. See also Shimazono, *Kokka Shintō to Nihonjin*, 56–58.

Some parts of this chapter are taken and/or edited from my earlier work, Kumada, "Theocracy and Constitutionalism in Japan".

3 Murakami, *Kokka Shintō*, 78–79; Shimazono, *Kokka Shintō to Nihonjin*, i, 35–39.
4 Murakami, *Kokka Shintō*, 134, 138; Shimazono, *Kokka Shintō to Nihonjin*, i.
5 Murakami, *Kokka Shintō*, 139–140; Shimazono, *Kokka Shintō to Nihonjin*, i–iii, 127–131, 146–148, 156–159.
6 Emiko Ohnuki-Tierney, *Kamikaze, Cherry Blossoms, and Nationalisms : The Militarization of Aesthetics in Japanese History* (Chicago: University of Chicago Press, 2002), 14.
7 Murakami, *Kokka Shintō*, 144.
8 Morihide Katayama and Susumu Shimazono, *Kindai Tennōron: "Shinsei" Ka "Shōchō" Ka* (Tōkyō: Kabushiki Kaisha Shūeisha, 2017), 82.
9 Historian Herbert Bix gives the following figures, though "the true dimensions of the human losses from World War II in Asia and the Pacific" are not known: China more than 10 million, the Philippines 1.1 million, Vietnam 1.5 to 2 million, Burma 150,000, Malaysia and Singapore more than 100,000, Koreas 200,000, and Taiwan 30,000; the number is unknown in Indonesia, but 4 million "forced laborers" suffered. Herbert P. Bix, *Hirohito and the Making of Modern Japan* (New York: Harper Perennial, 2016), 50.
10 The state also aestheticized state violence, although for space reasons this chapter cannot discuss the issue. See historian John W. Dower (2014) and anthropologist Emiko Ohnuki-Tierney's (2002) excellent works on this issue. See also Kumada (2018) on the way phrases such as a "beautiful" Japan is used as a code for *kokutai* in Japan today. John W. Dower, *Ways of Forgetting, Ways of Remembering: Japan in the Modern World*, Reprint edition (New York: The New Press, 2014); Ohnuki-Tierney, *Kamikaze, Cherry Blossoms, and Nationalisms*; Kumada, "Theocracy vs Constitutionalism in Japan".
11 Murakami, *Kokka Shintō*, 137; Shimazono, *Kokka Shintō to Nihonjin*, 36.
12 Shimazono, *Kokka Shintō to Nihonjin*, 36–38; Murakami, *Kokka Shintō*, 137–138.
13 Murakami, *Kokka Shintō*, 137; Shimazono, *Kokka Shintō to Nihonjin*, 37.
14 Morita Sutoppu, "Tsukamoto yōchien enji 'Abe sōri gabare! Abe sōri gabare!'" https://www.youtube.com/watch?v=5wV2BMqMi_I; Masoato Suzuki,

"Tsukamoto yōchienji ni yoru kyōikuchokugo anshō, saitamakengikai sasshin no kai shisatsu hen." https://www.youtube.com/watch?v=Wo_fxeRIER4.

15 See for example, Watanabe Tsutomu, "Kyōiku chokugo, naze kienu hyōka no koe moritomo mondai de chūmoku", Asahi Shimbun Digital, August 13, 2017, www.asahi.com/articles/ASK705RDYK70ULZU00P.html.

16 Nippon kyōiku gakkai, "Kyōiku chokugo no kyōzai shiyō ni kansuru kenkyū hōkokusho"; Kyōiku shigakkai rijikai, "'Kyōiku ni kansuru chokugo' (kyōiku chokugo) no kyōzai shiyō ni kansuru sēmē".

17 Ministry of Defence, "Defence Programs and Budget of Japan." https://www.mod.go.jp/j/yosan/2018/yosan.pdf; Cabinet Decision, "Kokka anzen hoshō senryaku ni tsuite." http://www.mod.go.jp/j/approach/agenda/guideline/pdf/security_strategy.pdf.

18 Kumada, "Theocracy vs Constitutionalism in Japan".

19 Murakami, *Kokka Shintō*, 80, 196; Shimazono, *Kokka Shintō to Nihonjin*, 143–144.

20 Murakami, *Kokka Shintō*, 206–207.

21 Masao Maruyama, *Gendai Seiji No Shisō to Kōdō* (Tōkyō: Miraisha, 1964), 15–17.

22 Katayama and Shimazono, *Kindai Tennōron*, 82.

23 Murakami, *Kokka Shintō*, 206.

24 Eiji Kosaka, "Yōchien no chōrei de kimigayo, kyōikuchokugo, (Shiritsu tsukamoto yōchien: Osaka-shi)." https://www.youtube.com/watch?v=oDfveoy1ixo; yawaraka4354, "[H24/02/16] Osaka Tsukamoto yōchien shisatsu." https://www.youtube.com/watch?v=0G_ujo_9sKA.

25 Murakami, *Kokka Shintō*, i.

26 Murakami, *Kokka Shintō*, iii; Shimazono, *Kokka Shintō to Nihonjin*, v.

27 Murakami, *Kokka Shintō*, 10, 132; Shimazono, *Kokka Shintō to Nihonjin*, 28–29, 166–167. See also Emiko Ohnuki-Tierney, *Kamikaze, Cherry Blossoms, and Nationalisms: The Militarization of Aesthetics in Japanese History* (Chicago: University of Chicago Press, 2002), 247.

28 Benedict R. O'G (Benedict Richard O'Gorman) Anderson, *Imagined Communities: Reflections on the Origin and Spread of Nationalism* (New York: Verso, 1991).

29 Maruyama, *Gendai Seiji No Shisō to Kōdō*, 162.

30 Compare this with the European case described by Kantorowicz. Ernst Hartwig Kantorowicz, *The King's Two Bodies [Electronic Resource]: A Study in Mediaeval Political Theology* (Princeton, NJ: Princeton University Press, 1997).

31 Maruyama, *Gendai Seiji No Shisō to Kōdō*, 14.

32 Ohnuki-Tierney, *Kamikaze, Cherry Blossoms, and Nationalisms*, 12; Murakami, *Kokka Shintō*, 7, 20, 31.

33 Murakami, *Kokka Shintō*, 69, 143; Ohnuki-Tierney, *Kamikaze, Cherry Blossoms, and Nationalisms*, 12.

34 Murakami, *Kokka Shintō*, 1, 24, 7, 122.

35 Murakami, *Kokka Shintō*, 1; Shimazono, *Kokka Shintō to Nihonjin*, 57–58.

36 Murakami, *Kokka Shintō*, 130; Shimazono, *Kokka Shintō to Nihonjin*, 7–18.

37 Murakami says that the idea that the Emperor is the father of all Japanese is based on the Confucius notion of loyalty and filial piety and the Japanese notion of ancestor worship. Ohnuki-Tierney has a different explanation, stating that it was borrowed from the foreign concept of "God the father". Murakami, *Kokka Shintō*, 137–138; Ohnuki-Tierney, *Kamikaze, Cherry Blossoms, and Nationalisms*, 12–13.

38 Ohnuki-Tierney, *Kamikaze, Cherry Blossoms, and Nationalisms*, 71–72, 79.

39 Murakami, *Kokka Shintō*, 118–19; Shimazono, *Kokka Shintō to Nihonjin*, 7–18.
40 Available in Japanese at: National Diet Library, "Dainippon tēkoku kenpō." https://www.ndl.go.jp/constitution/etc/j02.html. In English at: National Diet Library, "The Constitution of the Empire of Japan." https://www.ndl.go.jp/constitution/e/etc/c02.html.
41 Murakami, *Kokka Shintō*, 118–19; Shimazono, *Kokka Shintō to Nihonjin*, 7–10.
42 Murakami, *Kokka Shintō*, 159.
43 Maruyama, *Gendai Seiji No Shisō to Kōdō*, 13; Masao Maruyama, *Thought and Behavior in Modern Japanese Politics [Electronic Resource]* (New York: Oxford University Press, 1969), 3.
44 Maruyama, *Gendai Seiji No Shisō to Kōdō*, 13; Murakami, *Kokka Shintō*, 122.
45 Murakami, *Kokka Shintō*, 143; Maruyama, *Gendai Seiji No Shisō to Kōdō*, 13, 15, 17.
46 Maruyama, *Gendai Seiji No Shisō to Kōdō*, 15; Maruyama, *Thought and Behavior in Modern Japanese Politics [Electronic Resource]*, 8.
47 Maruyama, *Gendai Seiji No Shisō to Kōdō*, 15.
48 Maruyama, *Gendai Seiji No Shisō to Kōdō*, 157–158.
49 Murakami, *Kokka Shintō*, 139; Shimazono, *Kokka Shintō to Nihonjin*, 148.
50 Shimazono, *Kokka Shintō to Nihonjin*, 166–167.
51 Kōji Satō, *Sekaishi no nakano nihonkoku kenpō: Rikkenshugi no shiteki tenkai o fumaete* (Tōkyō-to Shibuya-ku: Sayusha, 2015), 14.
52 Satō, *Sekaishi no nakano nihonkoku kenpō: Rikkenshugi no shiteki tenkai o fumaete*, 14.
53 Satō, *Sekaishi no nakano nihonkoku kenpō: Rikkenshugi no shiteki tenkai o fumaete*, 14, 47, 50.
54 Shimazono, *Kokka Shintō to Nihonjin*, 66–67; see also Kōji Satō, *Rikkenshugi ni tsuite: sēritsukatē to gendai* (Tōkyō: Sayusha, 2015), 157, 159.
55 Shimazono, *Kokka Shintō to Nihonjin*, 176.
56 Takeshi Nakajima and Susumu Shimazono, *Aikoku to shinkō no kōzō: Zentai shugi wa yomigaerunoka* (Tokyo: Shūeisha, 2016), 124–130; Katayama and Shimazono, *Kindai Tennōron*, 147–149; see also Yuta Mizuuchi, "The Thought and Action of Kōdō Ōmoto: A Prehistory Authors", *The Zinbun Gakuhō: Journal of Humanities*, 108 (December 30, 2015): 85–96, https://doi.org/10.14989/204505.
57 Satō, *Sekaishi no nakano nihonkoku kenpō: Rikkenshugi no shiteki tenkai o fumaete*, 50.
58 Shimazono, *Kokka Shintō to Nihonjin*, 168.
59 Satō, *Sekaishi no nakano nihonkoku kenpō: Rikkenshugi no shiteki tenkai o fumaete*, 17; see also Satō, *Rikkenshugi ni tsuite: sēritsukatē to gendai*, 160.
60 Ohnuki-Tierney, *Kamikaze, Cherry Blossoms, and Nationalisms*; Emiko Ohnuki-Tierney, *Kamikaze Diaries: Reflections of Japanese Student Soldiers* (Chicago: University of Chicago Press, 2006).
61 Maruyama, *Gendai Seiji No Shisō to Kōdō*, 42–44, 161.
62 Maruyama, *Gendai Seiji No Shisō to Kōdō*, 161.
63 Nakajima and Shimazono, *Aikoku to shinkō no kōzō: Zentai shugi wa yomigaerunoka*.
64 Katayama and Shimazono, *Kindai Tennōron*; Satō, *Sekaishi no nakano nihonkoku kenpō: Rikkenshugi no shiteki tenkai o fumaete*, 47.
65 Maruyama, *Gendai Seiji No Shisō to Kōdō*, 291; see also Mizuuchi, "The Thought and Action of Kōdō Ōmoto: A Prehistory Authors".

66 Maruyama, *Gendai Seiji No Shisō to Kōdō*, 40; Maruyama, *Thought and Behavior in Modern Japanese Politics [Electronic Resource]*, 34–35.
67 Maruyama, *Gendai Seiji No Shisō to Kōdō*, 42; see also Murakami, *Kokka Shintō*, 138.
68 Maruyama, *Gendai Seiji No Shisō to Kōdō*, 42–43; Maruyama, *Thought and Behavior in Modern Japanese Politics [Electronic Resource]*, 36–37; see also Takeshi Suzuki, "The Cardinal Principles of the National Entity of Japan: A Rhetoric of Ideological Pronouncement", *Argumentation*, 15 (2001): 251–266.
69 Maruyama, *Gendai Seiji No Shisō to Kōdō*, 43–44.
70 A series of incidents took place from the League of Blood Incident (1932) up to the February 26 Incident (1936). Maruyama, *Gendai Seiji No Shisō to Kōdō*, 50; Maruyama, *Thought and Behavior in Modern Japanese Politics [Electronic Resource]*, 45; Satō, *Sekaishi no nakano nihonkoku kenpō: Rikkenshugi no shiteki tenkai o fumaete*, 14–17.
71 Maruyama, *Gendai Seiji No Shisō to Kōdō*, 50–51; Maruyama, *Thought and Behavior in Modern Japanese Politics [Electronic Resource]*, 196.
72 Maruyama, *Gendai Seiji No Shisō to Kōdō*, 51, 53.
73 Maruyama, *Gendai Seiji No Shisō to Kōdō*, 53.
74 Maruyama, *Gendai Seiji No Shisō to Kōdō*, 52–53.
75 Here, I borrow Gellner's distinction of the terms "patriotism" and "nationalism". Nationalism is a "distinctive species of patriotism". "[M]en have always lived in groups" and felt "loyalty" for and "identified with" these groups. On the other hand, nationalism "becomes pervasive and dominant only under certain social conditions, which in fact prevail in the modern world, and nowhere else". Ernest Gellner, *Nations and Nationalism* (Oxford, England: Blackwell, 1983), 137–143. See also Maruyama on the tension and gap between national consciousness and family-provincial consciousness. Maruyama, *Gendai Seiji No Shisō to Kōdō*, 161–164.
76 Maruyama, *Gendai Seiji No Shisō to Kōdō*, 44.
77 Shinto Directive (Shinto shirei): Kokka shinto, jinja shinto ni taisuru seifu no hosho, shien, hozen, kantoku, narabini kofu no haishi ni kansuru ken (Showa niju nen juni gatsu jugo nichi rengokokugun saiko shireikan soshireibu sanbo fuku kan . . . nihon seifu ni taisuru oboegaki).
In Japanese: www.mext.go.jp/b_menu/hakusho/html/others/detail/1317996.htm.
78 Mitsuhiko Sampa's report in Nippon kyōiku gakkai, "Kyōiku chokugo no kyōzai shiyō ni kansuru kenkyū hōkokusho" describes the process in detail. See also Watanabe, "Kyōiku chokugo, naze kienu hyōka no koe moritomo mondai de chūmoku".
79 Sampa; Watanabe.
80 Fujita, "Kyōiku chokugo, kyōzaika ni michisuji dainiji abe sēken de hyōka aitsugu". See also Watanabe.
81 Nippon kyōiku gakkai; Watanabe.
82 Nippon kyōiku gakkai; Watanabe.
83 Watanabe.
84 Watanabe.
85 Watanabe; Kumada, "Theocracy vs Constitutionalism in Japan".
86 Watanabe, "Kyōiku chokugo, naze kienu hyōka no koe moritomo mondai de chūmoku"; Fujita, "Kyōiku chokugo, kyōzaika ni michisuji dainiji abe sēken de hyōka aitsugu"; see also Kumada, "Theocracy vs Constitutionalism in Japan".
87 Ministry of Education, Culture, Sports, Science and Technology, "Kaisē zengo no kyōiku kihonhō no hikaku".

88 Watanabe, "Kyōiku chokugo, naze kienu hyōka no koe moritomo mondai de chūmoku".
89 *Seiron*, November 2007; Watabane.
90 Note the frequent appearance of the words describing love for the family, the provinces, and the country throughout the document: 3, 7, 13, 23, 25, 34, 36, 45, 46, 50, 51, 59, 91, 100, 109, 116. Ministry of Education, Culture, Sports, Science and Technology, "Shōgakkō gakushū shidō yōryō kaisetsu: Dōtoku hen", June 2008.
91 Groups of scholars and intellectuals express concern that pre-war moral education, including the teachings of the Imperial Rescript of Education, could be brought into the classroom as positive moral teachings. See the concerns expressed by various authors in the comprehensive report issued by Nippon kyōiku gakkai: 91, 96, 106, 108, 129, 134. See also Kyōiku shigakkai rijikai, "'Kyōiku ni kansuru chokugo' (kyōiku chokugo) no kyōzai shiyō ni kansuru sēmē".
92 In the earlier report by Nippon kyōiku gakkai, a chapter by Yoshikatsu Honda shows that a few of the new school textbooks positively evaluate the Imperial Rescript of Education, although the majority of the textbooks describe the Rescript critically.
93 Jiyū minshutō, "nihonkoku kenpō kaisē sōan".
94 "Kokka anzen hoshōsenryaku nit suite". Decenber 17, 2013.
95 Watanabe, "Kyōiku chokugo, naze kienu hyōka no koe moritomo mondai de chūmoku".
96 Maruyama, *Gendai Seiji No Shisō to Kōdō*, 154; Maruyama, *Thought and Behavior in Modern Japanese Politics [Electronic Resource]*, 137. Taken from translation by David Titus, with my minor edits.
97 Religious studies scholars have been warning their Japanese readers on the revival of State Shinto and totalitarianism. Murakami, *Kokka Shintō*, ii; Nakajima and Shimazono, *Aikoku to shinkō no kōzō: Zentai shugi wa yomigaerunoka*; Katayama and Shimazono, *Kindai Tennōron*. See also constitutional scholar Satō, *Rikkenshugi ni tsuite: sēritsukatē to gendai*, 220–221.
98 Nakajima and Shimazono, *Aikoku to shinkō no kōzō: Zentai shugi wa yomigaerunoka*; Satō, *Sekaishi no nakano nihonkoku kenpō: Rikkenshugi no shiteki tenkai o fumaete*, 90; Kumada, "Theocracy vs Constitutionalism in Japan".
99 See Abe's speeches for the October 2017 snap election and 2018 New Year. Kei Yoshikawa, "'Kokunan toppa kaisanda' abe shushōga kaisan o hyōmē. Kaiken de nani o katatta? [Zenbun]", *HuffPost Japan*, September 25, 2017, www.huffingtonpost.jp/2017/09/25/pm-abe_a_23221745/; Shinzō Abe, "Abe naikaku sōri daijin Heisei 30 nen nentō shokan", January 1, 2018, www.kantei.go.jp/jp/98_abe/statement/2018/0101nentou.html.

3 China's security imperatives and violence in Xinjiang

Stefanie Kam

Chinese officials' framing of Uyghur separatists as terrorists, and use of heavy-handed tactics under a broad counterterrorism template, is commonly assumed to have taken place in 2001. However, Beijing's current tactics, techniques and structures of governance in Xinjiang reflect continuity, rather than change, over the course of the past few decades. By examining new legal and discursive instruments, including the template of "strike hard" anti-crime campaigns beginning in the 1980s, and "Stability Maintenance" operations initiated in the mid-2000s, this chapter explores how Beijing has been able to rationalize and fortify its continued control over Xinjiang without changing its governmentality of Xinjiang.

This chapter first discusses the importance of Xinjiang to China, and the long-standing rebellions staged by Uyghur "separatists" (before 2001) and "terrorists" (after 2001). Furthermore, I also show how Beijing's policies of encouraging Han Chinese into Xinjiang to alter the ethnic composition there has been not only a side effect of its economic development policy in Xinjiang but also a governance technique used by Beijing to reinforce and reproduce existing patterns of governance. The next section explores the legal imperatives in Xinjiang since the 1980s as well as the political language of the "strike hard" campaigns of the 1980s. The third section reveals how public security officials throughout the 1980s and 1990s routinized and internalized its hard-line policing and security in a way that exemplified the state's paternalistic exercise of power. Finally, Beijing's securitization of Xinjiang shares two common elements: the first is the utilitarian dialectic of "striking hard" at Uyghur separatists, in contradistinction to the rest of society (the friend/foe dichotomy). The second is the paternalistic exercise of power by the state in a manner that warrants the use of incrementally intrusive cultural, religious restrictions, as well as visibly extensive stability maintenance measures and mechanisms. In this instance, paternalistic power functions to "discipline" Uyghur separatists who are deemed a threat, and to render "docile" members of the Uyghur community (including those deemed potential threats to the social stability and the authority of the Party-state) through governance of everyday life.

Situated close to Central Asia, Pakistan, and Afghanistan and occupying one-sixth of China, Xinjiang has a history of separatism that dates back to the rebellion in the mid-19th century led by Yaqub Beg, which saw an Islamic kingdom established in southern Xinjiang.[1,2] Xinjiang was formally absorbed by the imperial Qing rulers and declared a province in 1884, during the reign of the Manchu Qing Dynasty (1644–1911). After the Qing Empire's collapse, Xinjiang was immediately taken over by various warlords. Beijing's insecurities about the socio-political stability are informed by the fact that, in the 1930s and 1940s, Uyghurs set up two short-lived independent governments. The first was established in 1933 in the form of a Turkish Islamic Republic of Eastern Turkestan until it was crushed in 1934. In the fall of 1944, rebels backed by the Soviet Union carried out a revolt in the Ili prefecture, north of Xinjiang, establishing the second East Turkestan Republic. This second ETR was absorbed by the newly independent People's Republic of China (PRC). In 1967, at the height of the Sino-Soviet conflict, the East Turkestan People's Revolutionary Party (ETPRP), said to be one of the largest resistance organizations in Xinjiang since 1949,[3] sought to initiate a second uprising in Xinjiang similar to the one in 1944. In the 1970s, the Soviets also supported the United Revolutionary Front of East Turkestan (URFET), an armed resistance movement created to counter Chinese "oppression".[4]

In 1990, the "Islamic Party of East Turkistan", under Zeydin Yusuf's leadership, planned and executed a series of synchronized attacks on government buildings in what would culminate in the Baren Incident in southern Xinjiang. According to some reports, hundreds of people were killed in clashes with the Chinese police force. Rebels also seem to have propagated separatist ideologies and organized the rebellion through local mosques.[5] The official report on the incident stated that the group was "aided and abetted by the 'East Turkistan Islamic Party' . . . [and] brazenly preached a 'holy war', the 'elimination of pagans' and the setting up of an 'East Turkistan Republic'". In early 1997, a second riot took place in the city of Yining (Ghulja) as a response to the Strike Hard Campaign in 1996.[6] In early February 1997, Chinese authorities ordered the execution of 30 suspected separatists who had been involved in the organization of Meshrep during Ramadan. News spread to the city, provoking large demonstrations that eventually led to a riot. The Chinese government official figure for casualties of the riot was 198 injured and seven dead, while Uyghur exiles claimed up to 300 dead. The official report stated that "the 'East Turkistan

Party of Allah' and some other terrorist organizations perpetrated the Yining Incident, a serious riot during which the terrorists shouted slogans calling for the establishment of an 'Islamic Kingdom'".

Apart from the Uyghur ethnic minority, Xinjiang is home to 12 other ethnic groups—the Han, Kazak, Hui, Kyrghiz, Mongol, Xibe, Russian, Tajik, Uzbek, Tatar, Manchu, and Daur. According to the sixth census in 2010, the total population of Xinjiang was 3.11 million, with the Han accounting for 74.91% and the other ethnic minority groups accounting for 25.09% of the total population. When Xinjiang was declared an autonomous region in 1955, the chairman of the region's People's Council was a Uyghur named Seypidin Ezizi, while the top post in the regional military and Chinese Communist Party went to a Han general named Wang Enmao. This leadership pattern continues till today, with a Uyghur official holding symbolic control over Xinjiang but a Han Chinese official at the top of the hierarchy.

Foucault's notion of "pastoral power" provides the theoretical lens to understand China's tactics, techniques and structures of governance.[7] Embedded in the notion of pastoral power is the idea of "care" which is taken to mean the state's care for the welfare of its citizens. A similar idea can be found in the pastoral technique of governance within the ecclesiastical tradition of the Church, which is based on the relationship between the shepherd and his flock. The "shepherd-flock game" forms the basis for Foucault's conceptualization of power in modern-day societies, that which he calls the "city-citizen game". Although the state fundamentally exercises 'care' for the welfare of its citizens in both governing types, two tensions are inherent in the modern 'city-citizen game'. The first has to do with *the way power is exercised*, whether in the form of laws created through self-governing political communities, or in the form of concern for every member of the population, including individual existence or identity. The second deals with the *types of governed subject*, as this has to do with whether the individual is seen as a citizen, subject to legal and political rights and obligations, or a target of pastoral power, in which case, the citizen becomes both at once obedient (to the state) and needful (of its protection).[8]

The legal justification

China's legalization of its coercive use of force in the 1980s provided a legal basis for "the particular justification of state coercion".[9] This is with respect to its first "strike hard" campaign of "severe and swift" punishment introduced in 1983 which saw routine criminal justice operations shifted into a campaign mode of 'striking hard' expeditiously and with full force.

The logic of the campaign was to allow the state to use its authority to exact punishment using the full force of law and to shorten judicial proceedings. This punitive approach aimed at attacking the enemy was the dominant mode of the "strike hard" strategy. This strategy gained further salience in 2014 in the subsequent language of political struggle evinced under the campaign label of the "people's war on terror".[10] Coming on the heels of the terrorist attack at the busy street market in Urumqi and following Xi Jinping's speech the day before at the Central Work Forum in Xinjiang, the move exemplified the Chinese government's commitment to punish members of the public involved in these violent attacks severely. The speech also outlined plans for an assimilation policy to modify the attitudes and behaviours of Muslims in the region.[11]

In reality, this legal sleight of hand which Chinese authorities were able to invoke to bypass routine measures existed prior to the "strike hard" campaigns of the early 1980s, and in fact dates back to the early decades of the PRC's founding. In 1958, close to a decade after China was formally declared a single, unitary multiethnic state under the Chinese Communist Party, the Chinese government relied on leading small groups to coordinate and guide action on its internal security and stability, which mostly centred on counter-revolutionary forces. Such leading small groups were extra-ministerial and informally set up "to avoid the reach of legal reforms when dealing with a perceived existential threat to their power".[12] Thus, throughout the 1980s, even though China's legal counterterrorism apparatus remained underdeveloped, and Uyghur separatists were dealt with according to criminal laws, China managed the threat in a similar manner. This continued till around the 1990s, when new counterterrorism mechanisms were developed under the Ministry of Public Security (MPS). China also re-initiated "strike hard"/maximum pressure campaigns in the mid-1990s, mass arrests, razing of religious sites, indefinite detentions, executions and accelerated trials. This period saw the creation of a specialized unit called the Shanghai Special Weapons and Tactics Force. The late 1990s and early 2000s were marked by a centralization of the counterterrorism organs, and a wider range of counterterrorism approaches. The Shanghai Cooperation Organisation (SCO) was formed in 2001, and under the MPS, China created a National Counterterrorism Working and Coordinating Small Group (NCTWCSG) to centralize national counterterrorism efforts.

To guide China's anti-terrorism and national security work towards the formulation and implementation of an overall security strategy for the country, China established the National Security Council (NSC) on 12 November 2013.[13] The introduction of its new national security law in 2015 stretched the definition of "core interest" to encompass all sovereignty issues of salience to China.[14] In August 2015, China introduced several provisions on terrorism in its 9th Amendment to the Criminal Code and passed its first anti-terrorism law in December 2015, providing an explicit legal basis for the country's counterterrorism organs to suppress and prevent terrorist activities in the country.[15] The chapters on counterterrorism comprise the designation of terrorist organizations and personnel; security and prevention; intelligence information; investigation; response and handling; international cooperation; supportive measures; legal responsibility; and supplementary provisions.[16]

The counterterrorism law introduced in 2015 provided a broad definition of terrorism as "any advocacy or activity that, by means of violence, sabotage, or threat, aims to create social panic, undermine public safety, infringe on personal and property rights, or coerce a state organ or an international organisation, in order to achieve political, ideological, or other objectives". This definition provides a legal basis for China to adopt a variety of legal measures in addressing the threat of terrorism ranging from ordinary and quasi-criminal laws; focused provisions targeting specific security threats such as terrorist acts, separatism and sedition; to laws that authorize more radical departure from the usual legal rules. These include impositions of martial law, states of emergency and other legal states of exception.[17] A range of legal instruments has been invoked to deal with the unrest in Xinjiang, from ordinary criminal statutes proscribing violent acts, prosecutions under more specific provisions addressing terrorist, seditious and separatist acts, and renewed consideration of special emergency powers laws for the paramilitary police.

The moral justification

In the 1990s, the Chinese government introduced "stability maintenance" (*weiwen*) as a policy agenda.[18] China's framing of its response to unrest in Xinjiang in terms of the "stability maintenance" agenda occurred along the lines of its securitization of the Uyghur ethnic minority. Unlike the "strike hard" campaigns of the 1980s, "stability maintenance" entailed addressing both political control and economic development in Xinjiang with the goal of ensuring stability in the region. Cognizant of the intermestic nature of the security threat in Xinjiang—the separatist threat being entangled with the Central Asian countries—the state implemented a dual strategy. Firstly, it reinforced the importance of the party's control over the practice and influence of religion and religious activities in Xinjiang. Secondly it also implemented an economic development strategy which included the Central Asian states as partners. The purpose was to (1) focus on promoting development in Xinjiang by opening it to the Central Asian economies to reduce the regional disparities witnessed at that time, and (2) to stabilize the region by cooperating with the Central Asian states to reduce and prevent the spread of separatism and religious extremism. The importance of development to stability was not confined to Xinjiang, and it followed a policy trend that was already occurring in the rest of Mainland China during the 1990s. For instance, at the 14th Party Congress in 1992, Jiang Zemin, General Secretary of the Central Committee of the Chinese Communist Party (CCP), declared the importance of stability maintenance as an essential precondition for economic development.[19] In 1999, a top-level "Leading Small Group" was established to oversee stability maintenance.[20] Thus, the 2000 campaign to "Open Up the West"[21] functioned as a conduit for consolidating efforts throughout China, and in many respects fortified Chinese control of Xinjiang in the 21st century. As a model for the modernization and integration of its western regions, the State Council Committee for Developing the Western Region was set up in January 2000 and the following year a comprehensive 10th Five Year Plan (focusing on four general categories: infrastructure development, environmental protection, change to industrial structure and technology and education) was brought forward.[22]

By 2007, at the 17th Party Congress, in tandem with Hu Jintao's slogan of building a "harmonious society", stability maintenance became a national security priority and a principal objective in China's domestic security operations.[23] A consequence of this has been the implementation of new security measures and institutions, the establishment of "stability maintenance service centres" which were designed to not only coordinate efforts by local police stations, but also those dealing with the investigation and suppression of forbidden religious movements such as the Falungong, local courts and local units of the CCP. In parallel to such stability maintenance operations has been a corresponding "depersonalization" of power through the state's ability to keep every aspect of Xinjiang society within its optical reach. Thus, the emergence of expansive surveillance technologies in the 21st century has served to ensure the despotic exercise of power in the form of "care" is consciously internalized by its citizens. The use of propaganda and the presence of re-education camps and educational curriculum emphasizing Chinese socialist education has also functioned to erase ethno-nationalism and to reinforce the notion of the Chinese nation-state. In September 2009, the state issued a White Paper on the Development and Progress in Xinjiang[24] outlining the benefits of the development of the province under China's rule. According to the document, China has actively promoted ethnic equality and freedom of religion in Xinjiang and has fostered the Uyghur autonomy. While on paper China propagated autonomy, in reality, it imposed the policies of central control over religion, education and language in Xinjiang. As a form of "infrastructural power",[25] such a strategy functioned to bind Xinjiang's citizens closer to the Chinese state.

Finally, the Chinese government also resorted to propaganda to discursively construct a narrative which defined the continued maintenance of social order as a consequence of the CCP's authoritarian rule. This exemplifies the pastoral power of the state as a provider of security and stability. For instance, in 2015, China released a White Paper on the Historical Witness to Ethnic Equality and Development in Xinjiang in which the document offered glowingly positive reviews of the CCP's efforts in the region:

> Since the peaceful liberation of Xinjiang in 1949, and the founding of the Xinjiang Uygur autonomous region in 1955 in particular, Xinjiang has seen continued improvement in its standard of living, comprehensive progress in various areas, stability in the overall situation of society, and positive momentum for development. All this has been made possible by strong support from the state and other parts of the country, as well as by the concerted efforts of all of Xinjiang's ethnic groups.[26]

In a 2017 report on "Human Rights in Xinjiang—Development and Progress", Chinese officials stated that development policies in the region have helped the ethnic groups in Xinjiang, which include the Uyghurs, increase in social status. The report added that Xinjiang has seen a marked increase in GDP, from 3.9 billion yuan ($573 million) in 1978 to 961.7 billion yuan ($139.8 billion) in 2016.[27]

The ratcheting of legal and institutional means to securitize the region, maintain control over the religious and cultural lives of ordinary citizens in Xinjiang, and pronouncements of the benefits in Xinjiang under the CCP's rule exemplifies a form of power which combines the despotic (power over society) and infrastructural (power through society). As Mann explains, such a form of power "flows principally from the state's unique ability to provide a *territorially-centralised* form of organisation".[28] The incorporation of stability maintenance as a criterion for evaluating and promoting Party cadres in China, including those in Xinjiang, also turned stability maintenance, through a process of normalization, into a routinized mode of governance. An important implication of this has been the strengthening of the entire politico-legal apparatus of China, which in principle works under the framework of maintaining stability. In actuality, however, such operations served only to support the Chinese government's efforts at regime legitimation. In his 2014 visit to Xinjiang, President Xi Jinping stressed: "Xinjiang's social stability and its long-term stability concerns the relationship between the stability of China's overall development, reunification with the motherland, national unity, state security, and the great rejuvenation of China".[29] At the National Politico-legal Work Conference on 8 January 2014, Xi also declared that China's politico-legal organs needed to align their agendas more closely with the Party's current stability and security concerns. Xi called on greater coordination between the police, judges, prosecutors and security officials and referred to these organs as the Party's "dagger-handle" which the government would mobilize to respond swiftly and severely in instances of instability. Apart from employing the logic of stability maintenance to rationalize modifications to routine security procedures, the Chinese government also ensured the continual reproduction of the utilitarian logic of the "strike hard" campaigns. It did so through building a "partnership of stability" with the Han. Following the 2009 Urumqi riots, and following widespread Han complaints that the then-Xinjiang party chief had failed to protect them and their property and failed to "maintain stability" from the separatists, the Chinese government proceeded to remove the then-Xinjiang party chief, Wang Lequan. The newly assumed Xinjiang Party Secretary, Zhang Chunxian, continued to emphasize a utilitarian dialectic of "friend" versus "foe/enemy" and called for a people's war against terrorism to "exterminate" the "savage and evil separatists" who were influenced and directed by foreign "extremists".[30] After 2009, expansive measures were enforced in Xinjiang, in the form of raids on mosques, house-to-house searches by police and increased arbitrary arrests and executions throughout the year.[31] To stifle popular discourse which would undermine its rule in the months after the 2009 incident, China criminalized online discussions of separatism and shut down the Internet in Xinjiang following the incident.[32]

China's security and military institutions have played an important role in serving to legitimize its use of force in Xinjiang. The security arm of the Chinese government, comprising the civilian police, government security forces and military forces, is in charge of clamping down on dissent and responding to a range of uprisings and insurgencies. As a military, China's People's Liberation Army (PLA) is also equipped to deal with both external and internal threats and supports the Chinese state internally through conducting domestic security operations in exceptional circumstances. Since 1983, the Ministry of Public Security (MPS) has been responsible for enforcing the law and for exercising civilian control over the People's Armed Police (PAP), a domestic policing body comprising some 50,000 to 100,000 troops, many of whom were demobilized from the PLA. The Xinjiang Production and Construction Corps (XPCC), along with PLA and PAP forces, are responsible for cracking down on separatism and for acting as a non-coercive force for Xinjiang's economic and urbanization plans. Officially established in 1954 as a unit dominated by Han Chinese, the XPCC is charged with defending the border regions and assisting in the region's progression from a frontier of control to a frontier of settlement. As "the nucleus of stability in Xinjiang"[33] and an instrument of the state's paternalistic power, the continued relevance and survival of the XPCC hinges on the continued securitization of the threat of Uyghur separatism by the state.[34]

Since the 2009 Urumqi riots, there has been a considerable build-up of security and security innovation in Xinjiang. The Chinese government refers to this as a system of grid-style social management which is based on the idea of using high-tech surveillance techniques to govern the "possible fields of action". It included the use of CCTV cameras, mobile Internet technologies and big data analytics to monitor all activities within a discrete geometric zone. At least 90,000 police officers have been recruited in Xinjiang since 2009, where they are mobilized at convenience police stations. Surveillance cameras are deployed at the entrances of mosques throughout Xinjiang.[35] Patriotic slogans and the national flag sit atop the exteriors of mosques, seemingly to persuade non-Muslims of Muslims' patriotism and the acceptable position of Islam within the Chinese nation. They also function to convey a message to Muslims: that their agentive participation in establishing an independent East Turkestan separate from the Chinese nation-state is not only unwanted but impossible. Islamic inscriptions are prohibited to be on display in the mosques and in their place, China has instructed red banners to be hung. Apart from banners which read "Love the Party, Love the Country", flag-raising ceremonies are held at mosques, where the Chinese national anthem and a patriotic song ("Without the Communist Party, There Is No New China") is sung.[36]

The Uyghur ethnic minority's agitation for an independent "East Turkestan" has occurred alongside reports that Uyghurs have travelled the Middle East and have joined militant groups there.[37] Other Uyghurs have turned to using legitimate and democratic platforms as a resistance strategy.[38] The World Uyghur Congress (WUC) currently stands as the main advocacy group for Uyghurs, and has its headquarters in Munich, Germany. While most of the transnational human rights networks that are sympathetic towards the Uyghurs may not necessarily agree with the independence of Xinjiang, Uyghur rights groups support the independence of Xinjiang to varying extents.[39] Some media organizations have played a direct or indirect role in transnationalizing the Uyghur cause.[40]

Final reflections

Confronted by incidents of social unrest in the 1980s and Uyghur-related unrest and rising ethno-nationalist movements in the post-Soviet Central Asian republics in the 1990s, China utilized new legal and moral instruments to buttress its securitization of Xinjiang. Consequently, the state invested heavily in combating that which it deemed as real, urgent and incontestable sources of insecurity by expanding its security institutions, policies and operations. Fundamental to this process during the 1980s and beyond were two mutually reinforcing elements facilitating China's securitization of Xinjiang's Uyghurs: (1) a utilitarian dialectic, as seen in the "strike hard" campaign initiated in 1983 in which the repeated emphasis of a distinction between the friend (Han Chinese) versus foe/enemy (Uyghurs) legitimized the use of expedient and severe measures against the enemy; and (2) the state's paternalistic exercise of power, which was reflected in the exercise of "care" in the everyday lives of Uyghur communities. Ironically, this has only enabled Beijing to strengthen its core control over society.

During the 1980s, at the start of the "strike hard" anti-crime campaigns, using the utilitarian logic of "striking hard" the "foe/enemy", China was able to shift its criminal justice operations from routine processes into severe and swift operations in which the full force of law was meted out and judicial proceedings shortened. Essentially, this strategy of governing Xinjiang continued into the 1990s, but with some adjustments to its form. Faced with the threat of rising ethno-nationalism in the newly independent Central Asian republics and rising incidents of unrest internally, Chinese securitization of Xinjiang in the 1990s began under the broad banner of the "stability maintenance" agenda. Such a policy agenda offered a more nuanced modification (and indeed, retrospective justification) for its "strike hard" campaigns of the 1980s. Its utilitarian approach to punishment which distinguished the "friend" from the "foe/enemy" and otherized Uyghur separatists was informed by a logic of maintaining stability. This logic of maintaining stability justified the exercise of paternalistic power in all aspects of society, legitimizing Beijing's right to govern over the "productive" spaces in which Uyghurs inhabit. Religious and cultural restrictions were initiated. These took the form of the 1996 "strike hard" campaigns, which saw government crackdowns on illegal religious activities and the shutting down of private Quranic schools in the region. More intrusive and expansive measures and mechanisms of security were also implemented. These included the introduction of surveillance systems and the ratcheting of security personnel in the region, particularly after the 2009 Urumqi riots. These securitization processes occurred in parallel with Uyghur contestations and therefore fundamentally reveal an inherently asymmetrical power struggle between the Chinese securitizing state and its Uyghur ethnic minority constituents. Essentially, this power struggle reflects what Foucault refers to as a 'permanent provocation' in which relations between the securitizing actor and the securitized Uyghur separatists are sustained (and not negated) by the mutual existence of confrontation on both sides.

By exploring the politics of (in)security in Xinjiang, this study shows that China's legal and moral justifications were continuously informed by the state's understanding of its role as a paternalistic and pastoral guardian responsible for transforming the barbaric, uncivilized Other into its own image. Therefore, the consequentialist dimensions of China's security imperatives in Xinjiang have shaped the particularistic nature of the experiences of Xinjiang's Uyghurs. The findings reinforce the need to reconsider not only the use of legal and moral instruments as a means for the state to justify its securitization, but also as expressions of the state's own securitization practices.

Notes

1 Forbes, Andrew D. W. *Warlords and Muslims in Chinese Central Asia: A Political History of Republican Sinkiang 1911–1949*. Cambridge [Cambridgeshire]; New York: Cambridge University Press, 1986.
2 Guang, Pan. "China's Anti-Terror Strategy and China's Role in Global Anti-Terror Cooperation". *Asia Europe Journal* 2, no. 4 (December 1, 2004): 523–524. https://doi.org/10.1007/s10308-004-0115-7.
3 Wang, David D. "East Turkestan Movement in Xinjing". *Journal of Chinese Political Science* 4, no. 1 (June 1, 1998): 1–18. https://doi.org/10.1007/BF02876846.
4 Bovingdon, Gardner. *The Uyghurs: Strangers in Their Own Land*. New York: Columbia University Press, 2010.
5 Dillon, Michael. *Xinjiang: China's Muslim Far Northwest*. Durham East Asia Series. London; New York: Routledge Curzon, 2004, p. 73.
6 The 'strike hard' campaign of 1996 involved police crackdowns against what it deemed illegal religious activities and also the shutting down of private Quranic schools in the region.
7 Foucault, Michel, and Colin Gordon. *Power/Knowledge: Selected Interviews and Other Writings, 1972–1977*. New York ; Brighton, Sussex: Harvester, 1980.
8 Dean, Mitchell. *Governmentality: Power and Rule in Modern Society*. 2nd ed. Los Angles, CA; London: Sage, 2010, pp. 75–76.
9 Schmitt, Carl, and Jeffrey Seitzer. *Legality and Legitimacy*. Durham: Duke University Press, 2004, p. 4.
10 Trevaskes, Susan. "Using Mao to Package Criminal Justice Discourse in 21st-Century China". *The China Quarterly* 226 (June 2016): 304. https://doi.org/10.1017/S0305741016000266.
11 "张春贤：对暴恐分子不能实施仁政 只能高压严打--中国人大新闻--人民网". Accessed November 27, 2018. http://npc.people.com.cn/n/2014/0307/c376899-24565974.html.

Immediately after President Xi's Central Work Forum speech, senior Party leaders met to address the issue of stabilizing the situation in Xinjiang. Xinjiang Party Secretary Zhang Chunxian announced in a press release that, on 25 May, Party leaders had decided that police, prosecutors and judges would be required to switch into campaign mode, to conduct "hyper-hard-line operations" beyond the bounds of routine [justice system] measures.

12 An example of this is the 610 Office, which had its early beginnings in leading groups and functioned in 1999 to suppress the Falungong spiritual movement. See "The 610 Office: Policing the Chinese Spirit". Jamestown. Accessed November 27, 2018. https://jamestown.org/program/the-610-office-policing-the-chinese-spirit/; "To Rule China, Xi Jinping Relies on a Shadowy Web of Committees", *The Nerve Centre*. Accessed November 27, 2018. www.economist.com/china/2017/06/10/to-rule-china-xi-jinping-relies-on-a-shadowy-web-of-committees.

13 China's NSC deals with national security issues at home and abroad, and counterterrorism is a key organizational mandate.

14 "China Approves Sweeping Security Law, Bolstering Communist Rule", *The New York Times*. Accessed November 27, 2018. www.nytimes.com/2015/07/02/world/asia/china-approves-sweeping-security-law-bolstering-communist-rule.html; "Security Law Suggests a Broadening of China's 'Core Interests'", *The New York Times*. Accessed November 27, 2018. www.nytimes.com/2015/07/03/world/asia/security-law-suggests-a-broadening-of-chinas-core-interests.html.

15 "授权发布：中华人民共和国反恐怖主义法-新华网". Accessed November 27, 2018. www.xinhuanet.com/legal/2015-12/27/c_128571798.htm.

16 The law grants CCP the authority to compel the cooperation and assistance from technology firms and further enables the PLA or PAP to venture abroad in counterterrorism missions. The new Anti-Terrorism Act also provides another means of justifying surveillance of the Internet and electronic communications in China.

17 deLisle, Jacques. "Security First? Patterns and Lessons from China's Use of Law to Address National Security Threats". *Journal of National Security Law & Policy* 4, no. 2 (2010): 397–436. https://search-proquest-com.virtual.anu.edu.au/docview/872471484?accountid=8330.

18 The 'stability maintenance' policy gained prominence in the Chinese politico-legal spheres following the Tiananmen crackdown in 1989, the collapse of the Soviet Union in 1990 and after the Falungong threat in 1999. Following its initial conception, the stability agenda developed into a broader policy imperative combining the maintenance of law and order, surveillance, as well as the management of protests.

19 "Full Text of Jiang Zemin's Report at 14th Party Congress", *Beijing Review*. Accessed November 27, 2018. www.bjreview.com.cn/document/txt/2011-03/29/content_363504.htm.

20 Yuen, Samson. "The Politics of Weiwen: Stability as a Source of Political Legitimacy in Post-Tiananmen China". *European Consortium for Political Research (ECPR)*, (2014): 1–31. Accessed November 27, 2018. https://ecpr.eu/Events/PaperDetails.aspx?PaperID=16450&EventID=12.

21 The newly launched campaign in 2000 offered higher levels of urgency, investment and wider participation base, including Gansu, Guizhou, Ningxia, Qinghai, Shaanxi, Sichuan, Xinjiang, Yunnan and Chongqing.

22 Kerr, David, and Laura C. Swinton. "China, Xinjiang, and the Transnational Security of Central Asia". *Critical Asian Studies* 40, no. 1 (March 2008): 89–112. https://doi.org/10.1080/14672710801959174.

23 "Harmonious Society". Accessed November 27, 2018. http://cpcchina.chinadaily.com.cn/2010-09/16/content_13918117.htm.

24 "White Paper on Development and Progress in Xinjiang". Accessed November 27, 2018. www.chinadaily.com.cn/ethnic/2009-09/21/content_8717461_7.htm.

25 Mann, Michael. "The Autonomous Power of the State: Its Origins, Mechanisms and Results." *European Journal of Sociology / Archives Européennes de Sociologie* 25, no. 2 (November 1984): 185–213. https://doi.org/10.1017/S0003975600004239.

26 "Full Text: Historical Witness to Ethnic Equality, Unity and Development in Xinjiang". Accessed November 27, 2018. http://english.gov.cn/archive/white_paper/2015/09/24/content_281475197200182.htm.

27 "Government White Paper Hails Xinjiang Human Rights Progress", *Global Times*. Accessed November 27, 2018. www.globaltimes.cn/content/1049534.shtml.

28 Mann, Michael. "The Autonomous Power of the State: Its Origins, Mechanisms and Results". *European Journal of Sociology / Archives Européennes de Sociologie* 25, no. 2 (November 1984): 185–213. https://doi.org/10.1017/S0003975600004239.

29 "奋力建设团结和谐繁荣富裕文明进步安居乐业的社会主义新疆（深入学习贯彻习近平同志系列重要讲话精神）--时政--人民网". Accessed November 27, 2018. http://politics.people.com.cn/n/2014/0526/c1001-25062091.html.

30 "'Major-Victory' Claimed as Terror Crackdown Begins", *China Digital Times (CDT)*. Accessed November 27, 2018. https://chinadigitaltimes.net/2014/05/major-victory-claimed-xinjiang-yearlong-terror-crackdown-begins/.

31 Grant, Peter, and Minority Rights Group. *State of the World's Minorities and Indigenous Peoples 2015: Events of 2014: Focus on Cities*. London: Minority Rights Group International, 2015.

32 Moore, Malcolm. "China Makes It Illegal to Discuss Independence for Xinjiang", September 28, 2009, sec. World. www.telegraph.co.uk/news/worldnews/asia/china/6239309/China-makes-it-illegal-to-discuss-independence-for-Xinjiang.html.

33 Cliff, Thomas. "The Partnership of Stability in Xinjiang: State-Society Interactions Following the July 2009 Unrest". *The China Journal* no. 68 (2012): 81.

34 It is significant that the *bingtuan* also existed in China's other regions in the 1970s, but with the exception of the Xinjiang *bingtuan*, were subsequently abolished in 1975.

35 "Xinjiang's Rapidly Evolving Security State", *Jamestown*. Accessed November 27, 2018. https://jamestown.org/program/xinjiangs-rapidly-evolving-security-state/.

36 Zhang, Xiaoling, Melissa Shani Brown, and David O'Brien. "'No CCP, No New China': Pastoral Power in Official Narratives in China". *The China Quarterly* 235 (September 2018): 784–803. https://doi.org/10.1017/S0305741018000954.

37 "Syria Says up to 5,000 Chinese Uighurs Fighting in Militant Groups", *Reuters*. Accessed November 27, 2018. www.reuters.com/article/uk-mideast-crisis-syria-china/syria-says-up-to-5000-chinese-uighurs-fighting-in-militant-groups-idUSKBN1840UP.

38 Clarke, Michael. "China, Xinjiang and the Internationalisation of the Uyghur Issue". *Global Change, Peace & Security* 22, no. 2 (June 2010): 213–229. https://doi.org/10.1080/14781151003770846.

39 Chen Yu-Wen, Transporting Conflicts via Migratory Routes: A Social Network Analysis (SNA) of Uyghur International Mobilisation, NTS-Asia Research

Paper No. 5, Singapore: RSIS Centre for Non-Traditional Security (NTS) Studies for NTS-Asia.

40 Chen, Yu-Wen. *The Uyghur Lobby: Global Networks,Coalitions and Strategies of the World Uyghur Congress*. Routledge Contemporary China Series. London; New York: Routledge, 2014, pp. 117–118. https://virtual.anu.edu.au/login/?url=www.tandfebooks.com/isbn/9781315885421.

4 From pacifism to violence in Buddhist Myanmar

Jennifer Dhanaraj

While Myanmar is one of the most ethnically diverse and complex countries in the world, ethnic identity has often been politicized. The politicization of ethnic identity can be traced back to the British colonization of Burma from the early 1800s to 1948 during which the British often pursued policies along ethnic lines.[1] The colonial rulers documented the different ethnicities for administrative reasons that helped manage the population effectively.[2] The British established a two-tiered system, which was used to divide and rule colonial Burma: "Ministerial Burma" and "Frontier Areas". "Ministerial Burma" consisted of the majority Bamar ethnicity while "Frontier Areas" comprised ethnic minorities. Different authorities essentially ruled the two tiers—Ministerial Burma was ruled under a limited form of self-government while the British governor through hereditary ethnic minority leaders directly governed the Frontier Areas. This resulted in both areas developing at different rates and this further concretized and highlighted the various differences between the different ethnic identities. This was further exacerbated by the presence of Muslim immigrants from South Asia. Their arrival was welcomed by the British colonial powers, and the majority Bamar Burmese often felt that the growth of these communities resulted in the economic detriment of the Bamarese especially as Muslim South Asians came to take up prominent roles in important sectors like agriculture, transportation, merchants, moneylenders, and the British military and civil service.

The opposition to British rule then largely took the form of Bamar nationalism. Anti-colonial strikes, for example, led by Bamar resistance movements, often featured slogans like "Burma for Burmans" and "Master Race We Are, We Burmans". At the onset of World War II, Bamar nationalist groups allied themselves with the Japanese in the hope that the Japanese would force the British and their favored non-Bamar ethnic groups as well as South Asian communities out of Myanmar.[3] Upon independence, the Panglong Conference and Agreement of 1947 was supposed to represent an inclusive forum for ethnic groups to determine their united political objectives for independence.[4] However, many minorities were not represented. Additionally, policies were increasingly "Burmanized", which resulted in ethnic unrest. The introduction of the 1948 Citizenship laws defining indigenous races came into effect. But this was replaced in 1982 with a new nationality law allowing the State Council the right to determine who qualifies as "national race". People belonging to the 135 determined races are entitled to citizenship and rights but those outside of these races are not viewed as citizens. This includes descendants of migrants—often Muslim South Asians—and those of mixed ethnicity.

The colonial-era resentment of the Muslims continues today where Rakhine State is the forefront of violence between Buddhists and Muslims. Historically, the Rakhine majority has resented the presence of Rohingyas. There is also widespread public hostility towards the Rohingya in Myanmar because they are not viewed as being a true citizen of Myanmar. This is supported by the country's constitution that does not include Rohingyas among the indigenous groups that qualify for citizenship. The minority Muslim population in Rakhine State continues to stoke fears within the local Buddhist population and fears of an "invasion" by Muslim immigrants have been prevalent since the colonial era where the British encouraged immigrants from Bangladesh to work in Myanmar. As such, Buddhists in Rakhine have always believed that it is their duty to protect and defend the "western gate" of the country against such an invasion. This need to protect the country from "the other" has then extended throughout the country—as can be seen in the anti-Muslim violence that continues to plague Myanmar. In June 2012, waves of deadly violence erupted in Rakhine State. The catalyst of this wave was the rape and murder of a young Buddhist woman by a Muslim man. This sparked widespread rioting and clashes between Rakhine Buddhists and Muslims, who were mostly Rohingya Muslims. This initial wave left almost 200 dead and displaced thousands more. Since then, the violence against Muslims has spread across Myanmar, as can be seen in the 2013 anti-Muslim riots that swept central Myanmar as well as Mandalay. In March 2013, an argument in a gold shop in Meiktila in central Myanmar led to violence between Buddhists and Muslims, which left more than 40 people dead and entire neighborhoods razed.[5]

The violence reached a new peak in 2017 when Rohingya militants attacked government forces on August 25. In response, security forces supported by Buddhist militia have undertaken what the international media and organizations refer to as an "ethnic cleansing operation". The UN's top human rights official said on 11 September that the military's response was disproportionate to the earlier insurgent attacks and the treatment of the Rohingya minority appears to be a "textbook example" of ethnic cleansing.

This has prompted Buddhists elsewhere in the country to perpetrate acts of violence against Muslims. In September 2017, a mob in the Magway region in central Myanmar stoned the home of a Muslim butcher. A 400-strong crowd sang the national anthem and lobbed rocks at the butcher's home before heading over to the local mosque. That the mob purposefully targeted a Muslim man and sang the national anthem indicate that they are justifying their use of violence by normalizing and moralizing it, as their violence against "the other" is seen as a duty to protect their nation—and therefore their religious identity. A common narrative that is often repeated across Myanmar is that the country would have turned to Islam long ago if Buddhists did not defend and protect Rakhine State or "western gate" from an invasion by the Muslim immigrants from Bangladesh. As such, Buddhists believe that it is their duty to protect their religion by ensuring that the rest of Myanmar (outside of Rakhine State) holds strong against demographic changes that would favor the Muslims.[6] This duty to protect Buddhism from the other has resulted in communal violence against Muslims becoming more widespread across Myanmar as well. Beyond these demographic pressures, however, lies a fear that more Muslims in the rest of Myanmar would mean that Muslims will hoard capital and buy up crucial real-estate as well as marrying Buddhist women and coercing them to convert to Islam. This sentiment is strikingly similar to the rhetoric used against Indians (many of whom were Indians) in the colonial era where there was a popular song from the 1930s borne out of the Burmese nationalist movement. This song had lyrics saying that Indians were "exploiting our resources and seizing our women, we are in danger of racial extinction".[7] Once again, there is the recurrent theme of a race (or religion) being driven to decline—or even worse, extinction.

Identity, religion, and violence

To understand why Buddhist extremists in Myanmar are eager to demonize the "other" and construct narratives of evil to justify the violence, one has to look into their fear of negation. Buddhists consider their identity to be intricately and intimately linked with their national identity.[8] This fear of servitude can be understood by drawing upon the Hegelian master-slave dialectic framework. An important aspect of this framework is the idea that the identity of the self must remain distinct, yet equally significant to the other. In *The Essence of Islamist Extremism*, Irm Haleem argues that self-recognition in the radical Islamist context has tended to be marked by violence. Haleem draws upon Axel Honneth's work in *The Struggle for Recognition: The Moral Grammar of Social Conflicts*, which argues that morality is re-presented as actions that seek respect and honor for the self. As such, the struggle for recognition for the self is seen as a quest for morality and is thus framed in moral language.[9] Essentially, the struggle for recognition leads to a consequentialist notion of morality. For example, any action that rejects the negation of one's identity is seen as moral as it achieves the intended consequence of recognition. Therefore, moral consequential reasoning serve as explanations of violence and are then buoyed by existentialist reasons such as the need for self-preservation of the self through gaining respect and dignity, which is defined as "right" in moral terms. Disrespect and marginalization then becomes "wrong" and therefore immoral.

Religious violence is used for consequentialist reasons to gain recognition for the self, which is often presented as a collective. However, to justify these actions, these consequentialist notions of morality are disguised as a religious imperative. In other words, the desire for recognition is seen as moral because it is a duty to God.[10] Recognition, which is existential in nature, is not just a sense of self-preservation. Instead, it refers to a sense of self-assertion and self-domination. Haleem refers to Nietzsche's will-to-power to illustrate this point. Will-to-power can be explained by how human behavior is driven by a domination or mastery of the others. She writes that since morality is a will-to-power, the desire for self-assertion and domination is existential in nature—and therefore a moral struggle. "If the will-to-power is the desire to dominate and the desire for self-assertion, and if morality is a will-to-power, then this means that notions of morality are instrumental for the individual (or individuals) with a will-to-power; or, to put it in other words, the desire to dominate and the desire for self-assertion determine notions of morality", writes Haleem.[11] These notions of morality are consequentialist in nature because their aim is actually a desire for recognition. However, to hide any vested self-interests, morality is often presented under a deontological façade to add more urgency and legitimacy.[12] This ensures that the self understands that this struggle for recognition is one that requires quick, decisive actions that will fulfill a sense of duty. By framing it in deontological terms, any action to triumph in this struggle is seen as moral. Rightness or wrongness of the actions is therefore determined on whether the duty is fulfilled. Therefore, by presenting the struggle for recognition as a moral quest, any action to triumph in this struggle is seen as gaining respect and asserting domination over the master. Through this act of achieving victory, self-domination and self-assertion are then seen as fulfilling a duty. In this regard, religion is an important instrument as it frames the moral consequential explanations for violence as a sacred, divine duty.[13] Violence is justified as something that is moral because it is perceived to be fulfilling a duty.

In Myanmar, where the majority Bamar Burmese consider their identity to be intricately linked to Buddhism, desires for recognition become at once consequentialist and deontological. Buddhists consider their identity to be their national identity as a result of religion and its adherents introduced during the nation-state building process upon independence from the British in 1948.[14] This means that any attack on the nation is an attack on Buddhism and any attack on Buddhism is construed as an attack on the nation. In Myanmar, Buddhist extremists perceive the higher visibility of Islam and violence committed by Muslims as an attack on Buddhism as well as an attack on their nation. Buddhist extremists therefore see themselves as under threat. In an interview with CNN, a Bamar Buddhist Tin Win said, "They are expanding. They produce so many kids, so many children".[15] This statement points to a fear of an existential threat faced by Buddhists in Myanmar. The presence of Islam is seen as a direct threat to Buddhism. In fact, they fear that their religion (and therefore, nation) is in decline. Therefore, they have to struggle for recognition, which is the domination over the threat. Indeed, self-domination and self-assertion are the only way to neutralize the threat and survive. This view that Buddhism is under threat is a belief shared among many Myanmar Buddhists—especially since Myanmar's political opening in 2011 that has brought about a marked rise in Buddhist nationalism. Long-held grievances emerged into the open and political reforms in Myanmar allowed individuals to air their grievances with the various ways to exercise their right to freedoms of expression.

Additionally, the opening up of Myanmar coincided with the availability of telecommunications with access to the Internet and especially social media. This further amplified the threat posed by the Muslims and a significant proportion of Myanmar's Buddhist population felt this threat. When the self (or the collective self, in this case) feels threatened, they also feel inferior and they fear being a slave to a master. In other words, they fear servitude at the hands of the Muslims, who are perceived to be taking over the country by ensuring that Buddhism erodes. Bamar Buddhists therefore perceived themselves as slaves and used violence against Muslims as a tool to gain recognition. Therefore, the Buddhists' violence against the Muslims can be seen as symbolizing violence against the masters, who were often physically superior. The Bamar Buddhist feared oppression, humiliation, and especially servitude at the hands of Muslim South Asians, who were seen by the Bamarese to have some power, because they held key roles.[16] Only by achieving such superiority and dominance can the Buddhists shed their identity as a slave. Violence is therefore the only path to achieve such mastery and dominance over the other in order to gain recognition. As this is an existential struggle in itself to protect their identity, and more importantly, religion, any acts of violence to gain victory in this struggle is therefore seen as moral—because these acts, while intended to achieve recognition, are perceived as fulfilling a duty to God.

When the struggle for recognition is moralized, violence is therefore normalized. As a result, the proliferation of narratives that painted Islam and Muslims as threatening Buddhists and Buddhism has led to Buddhist extremists' desire for recognition, which is seen as a moral act in itself. This has further intensified the wave of anti-Muslim violence that continues to sweep across the country.

Construction of evil: Or justifying violence as morality

David Frankfurter writes that religion provides symbols and imagery, which are tools necessary to create an evil that must be fought and overcome.[17] Buddhist extremists' desire for recognition is disguised as the fight for the survival of their religion. To further legitimize and moralize this violence, this struggle is presented as "good vs. evil". When you are fighting something that is considered to be evil, violence is sanctioned and indeed necessitated, as evil has to be destroyed at all cost. Good has to triumph over evil—and to realize that is to fulfill your duty. An effective way to create an evil is therefore to project religious imagery and symbols onto the "other". A common narrative used by Buddhist extremists to cast Muslims as evil is to repeat the rhetoric that Muslim men rape Buddhist women in every town.[18] This statement is often accompanied with religious undertones. The rhetoric of Muslims raping Buddhist women suggests that Muslims are infecting the purity of the Buddhist religion. Additionally, Buddhist extremists have said that the goal of the Muslims is to overpopulate the nation with Muslims. Again that implies that Muslims, and Islam, are seen as an impurity that needs to be purged. The construction of evil involves creating narratives of "the other" as "evil" and this is often based on exaggerations. This is done for several purposes: such as the massification of the "other" which further makes it easier to demonize the "other". When all Muslims are presented as evil, it is morally much easier to perform acts of violence indiscriminately. Essentially, the construction of evil by Buddhist extremists has utilized religion to reframe the community's social reality so that Muslims are presented as the "evil" as opposed to the "good" that the Buddhists represent. When the struggle for recognition is framed in a language that invokes ritual practices and purification rights, it further justifies the urgent need for violence—and even moralizes it. After all, what good is being good if you are not overcoming evil?[19] The construction of evil therefore provides a moral catalyst and a justification for violence as it is presented as the only way to overcome and purge the impurity. To do so, Buddhist extremists turn to divine texts and highlight the appropriate imagery to reiterate the clear divide between good and evil—and more importantly, the duty of Buddhists to ensure that good triumphs over evil.

The Pali Canon, the standard collection of scriptures in the Theravada Buddhist tradition, provides key insight into the central teachings of Buddhism, and is the text that is often memorized and recited by monks. There are five precepts for conduct (in the Theravada tradition—the predominant practice in Myanmar) that had been codified throughout Buddhism's history. The first of which is to abstain from taking life.[20] The Buddha insisted on this and said in the scripture: "Conquer the angry man by love; conquer the ill-natured man by goodness; conquer the misery with generosity; conquer the liar with truth". There are also no heavenly rewards for those who commit acts of violence in the name of the Three Jewels—Buddha, Dharma (teaching of the Buddha), Sangha (community who follows the teaching).[21] However, in several scriptures, these rules can be bent based on several variables. Some of the more popular exceptions are, as Michael Jerryson wrote, "the nature of the victim, the intentions behind the act of killing and the stature of the one who kills". These exceptions are crucial for the construction of evil that helps to justify the acts of violence by Buddhist extremists against the "other".[22]

In this regard, that Buddhist monks, dressed in their symbolic Saffron robes, in Myanmar are often creating narratives to construct evil further serves to mobilize people to commit acts of violence to protect the religion from unwelcomed, possibly, contaminated influences that can threaten the survival of the religion. This can be seen in the rhetoric from leaders of Myanmar's 969 movement as well as Ma Ba Tha (Association for the Protection of Race and Religion). Ashin Wirathu, a Buddhist monk, is widely seen as the extremist leader behind the anti-Muslim movement in Myanmar. Wirathu has, since 2001, preached anti-Islam messages that often demonize Muslims. He preaches these messages in his sermons. He constantly says that Islam threatens Buddhism (even though Islam represents only 5 per cent of Myanmar's population) and therefore "the very essence of Myanmar".[23] So his actions are perceived as being tantamount to protecting the religion and nation. In a 2013 sermon, Wirathu made a clear divide between Burmese Buddhists (the collective self) and the Muslims (the other). He said that it was important for the Buddhist public to adopt a nationalist mindfulness where they have to "eat, sleep, hear, speak and breathe" Buddhist nationalism. He also referred to a common theme in his sermons: the "population explosion" in Rakhine State. Wirathu says that because Muslims men can have more than one wife, it will lead to a population explosion and they will be able to capture "our country" in the end. This is a clear exaggeration of facts that is meant to construct the image of Muslims in Myanmar as invaders seeking to disrupt the Buddhists' way of life. He also accuses the government of failing to protect Burmese Buddhists from Muslims.

Crucially, Wirathu invokes religious symbols and elements to further push the narrative of "the other" and to push the urgency of the need to deconstruct that evil by taking action. In the same 2013 sermon, he refers to the meaning of 969. Wirathu says: "We [referring to Burmese Buddhists] must all adopt this "969" Buddhist nationalist mindfulness; 9 stands for the nine special attributes of Lord Buddha; 6 for the special attributes of his teaching/Dharma; and 9 for the nine special attributes of the Sangha or Buddhist Order". [24] According to Frankfurter, the use of such religious symbolism further bolsters the narrative that only emphasizes the bad that 'the other' does.[25] Wirathu also tends to deliver his sermons in a calm, steady manner, as he rocks back and forth as he holds on to the Buddhist prayer beads (mala). In his compound that is within the Masoeyein monastery in Mandalay, there is a wall of photos depicting brutal, grotesque injuries including disfigured faces and slashed bodies. Wirathu claims that the victims are Buddhists and that they were attacked by Muslims. Once again, it shows how religious institutions can play a big role in popularizing "an official demonology".[26] This demonology can be embedded within an ideology that can resonate with the masses and therefore mobilize them—especially if their worldview is grounded by sacred images and ideas.[27] Those who are heavily informed by such a worldview may in turn legitimize violence because religion can be seen as an absolute truth. This worldview—that is bolstered by the construction of evil—presents violence as a morality. Additionally, when religious leaders like Buddhist monks create norms and dispense them through a narrative, they are deciding what morality is going to be and so the masses tend to uncritically accept those notions of morality and accept that violence is indeed moral to deconstruct the evil. Violence is then justified based on the just-war doctrine—specifically self-defense.

Identity, evil, and self-defense

This concept of self-defense is very prevalent in the narratives constructed on social media networks like Facebook, which is extremely popular in Myanmar. Facebook is also widely believed to be the only forum of discourse for people in Myanmar—it is also widely trusted as a source of news and information.[28] Extremist leaders, like Wirathu, often take advantage of this and spread disinformation and utilize Facebook to spread such polarizing messages that further fuel hate and make Burmese Buddhists feel like they have to resort to violence to protect their people and religion. Stories spread by Wirathu include pictures of dead bodies that he claimed were killed by Muslims.[29] Other Buddhist nationalist monks have also relied on

Facebook to construct this evil (some have dehumanized Muslims by comparing them to dogs) to further mobilize people to incite violence against "the other". This construction of evil then makes it easier to justify violence especially when used together with holy texts. If Buddhists commit acts of violence with the primary intention to save their religion from "evil", then the act of killing may not produce negative karma. So when "the other" is demonized, it also serves to justify the act of violence according to God.[30] In Buddhist scriptures, there is the concept of intention (*cetana*) where it is the intention of the act that matters. So if the intention is to protect the religion, acts of violence are justified according to God and are therefore legitimate. This is especially evident in the Myanmar Buddhists' acceptance and validation of the 969 movement—especially after it was banned by the Sangha Council, which is the government-appointed body of monks that oversees and regulates the Buddhist clergy. The 969 movement rejected the ban, claiming that the Sangha Council was formed by the state to serve the interests of the government and not Buddhism. This gave prominence to Ma Ba Tha as its nationalist ideology and its rallying call for the adoption of the race and religion laws were spread to the rural and remote parts of the country. Maintaining Buddhist cultural values is crucial to preserve the social and spiritual health of the religion and community at large. With groups like Ma Ba Tha claiming to do just that, Buddhists are more inclined to be receptive towards their ideology and be mobilized as a result. This is especially so as they see the government as incapable of defending and protecting their religion, especially after the government's rhetoric on the need for democratic pluralism and equality when referring to the Rohingyas. Many see this rhetoric as an affront to the religion and so believe that the government is not able to preserve the religion. Buddhist extremist groups are able to use their "moral authority" within the Myanmar Buddhists to further mobilize them and therefore normalize and moralize any violence against Muslims.

Religion offers a resonating ideology that mobilizes people because it offers a reasoning that few people dare to criticize. It exploits opportunities (local grievances and fears) and it allows religious leaders to effectively utilize their resources (good reputation, ideology, physical gathering space like monasteries) to further mobilize people and politicize religion by moving it from a private realm to a public realm.[31] Buddhist extremists often use grievances that appeal to all strata of Buddhist society—decline of the Buddhist religion so that it reaches the maximum number of people. By exploiting these opportunities and utilizing these resources with religion as a resonating ideology, religious leaders offer a moral justification to their followers—and present the need to commit acts of violence as a divine, God-given duty and this legitimizes that violence. This ideological resonance also makes people be part of a group and therefore, as a follower, you are responsible for the collective, which again gives followers a sense of duty. This is clear in rhetoric from Buddhist extremists in both Sri Lanka and Myanmar where they often cite the decline of religion and therefore the decline of economic opportunities, and free speech among others. By using religion to resonate with the masses, they are making their followers be part of a collective that has a duty to protect their religion and therefore acts of violence are tolerated. This can be seen in how Wirathu's speech in September 2012 incited many of his followers to riot in Meiktila, a city in central Myanmar. A mosque was burned to the ground and there were over a hundred dead. When followers believe they are fulfilling God's duty, they perceive these acts of violence as legitimate and as John Hall writes, further encourages a more dichotomous view of the world (sacred vs. profane where the sacred represents morality).[32] By presenting a narrative that the Buddhism religion is under threat, it presents an "Us ***OR*** Them" situation where as a member of the collective group, you have to do everything within your power to act. This is in line with Vamik Volkan's thinking on group conflict where the individual self equates his identity with the group identity.[33]

Volkan's thinking is also further reflected in the expectations that Burmese Buddhists have of their government. While international human rights groups as well as the international community at large pressure the government of Myanmar, more specifically Nobel Prize–winner Aung San Suu Kyi, many Burmese Buddhists believe that the Myanmar government should protect Myanmar and since being Burmese is equated to being Buddhist, many Burmese are calling for the government to prioritize the "protection" of Buddhism and prevent it from being weakened by the perceived "Islamic threat". This means that any national effort to stop the violence against the Rohingya people in Rakhine State can be seen as an action tantamount to letting Islam encroach on the rest of Myanmar. Violence is therefore seen by the Burmese Buddhists as a national security issue—an issue of survival. This is made even more clear as Burmese Buddhists seem to yearn for national policies that veer toward Buddhist nationalism and of clamping down on religious freedom for the minority.[34] This reflects Volkan's thinking that Burmese Buddhists see themselves as part of a collective group that needs to be protected—and so they view their government as the ones to 'protect' Buddhism from any group that may be perceived as threatening their group tent. Additionally, when they see themselves as part of a collective group, these members do not act as an individual entity. Instead, they act on behalf of a collective identity—collective self, if you will. This is further exemplified in footage of communal violence by Buddhists against Muslims that show Burmese Buddhists burning down mosques and looting stores belonging to Muslims and perpetrating violent acts against Muslims while chanting "Muslims are not Burmese".[35] As Muslims appear to threaten the group tent, they have to protect their collective group and the only tool is violence.

Final reflections

By denying Rohingyas citizenship, and excluding them from the 2014 census, thereby negating them, Myanmar propagates the narrative that the Rohingya Muslims are in fact the other. Such official otherizing gives a signal to Buddhist extremists that any violence perpetrated against the other is justified, and, indeed, moral. This is further evident in the fact that the government has consistently refused to acknowledge the military's role in the ethnic cleansing campaign against Rohingya Muslims. The government has only fired one general with regards to this campaign. The military continues to perpetuate false narratives about the Rohingya. As recently as August 2018, a new book on the Rohingya crisis has been written and published by the army's department of public relations, in which psychological warfare was used with fake photographs and key aspects of history were rewritten to justify the killings of Rohingyas. For example, in the book is a photograph showing a man wielding a farming tool as he stands over two bodies. The caption states that the image showed Buddhists murdered by Rohingya during ethnic riots in the 1940s. However, the photograph was actually taken during Bangladesh's 1971 independence war when hundreds of thousands of Bangladeshis were killed by Pakistani troops. By constructing and concretizing the narrative that Rohingya Muslims are the "other", it extends the narrative to Muslims across Myanmar, thereby further fueling mistrust between the two religions. Furthermore, while the government-appointed Sangha Council has effectively banned the 969 movement, it has failed to take on a stronger stance against violent Buddhist extremism. Instead of denouncing Ma Ba Tha's inflammatory anti-Muslim rhetoric and subsequent outbreaks of deadly violence, it merely focused on the movement's unauthorized use of Buddhist symbolism instead of rebuking its ideology. This has further given Ma Ba Tha and other Buddhist extremist groups more religious authority and so it has become easier to mobilize Buddhists with their ideology and then normalizing and moralizing violence.

Notes

1 Engy Abdelkader, "The History of the Persecution of Myanmar's Rohingya", *The Conversation*, accessed September 24, 2018, http://theconversation.com/the-history-of-the-persecution-of-myanmars-rohingya-84040

2 Matthew J. Walton, "The 'wages of Burman-Ness,'" *Journal of Contemporary Asia* 43:1 (2012).
3 Abdelkader, "The History of the Persecution of Myanmar's Rohingya".
4 Ye Htut, "Myanmar's Long Journey to Peace Starts in Panglong", *The Straits Times*, August 31, 2016, www.straitstimes.com/opinion/myanmars-long-journey-to-peace-starts-in-panglong
5 BBC News, "Why Is There Communal Violence in Myanmar", *BBC News*, July 3, 2014.
6 International Crisis Group, *Asia Report No. 290: Buddhism and State Power in Myanmar*, September 5, 2017, www.crisisgroup.org/asia/south-east-asia/myanmar/290-buddhism-and-state-power-myanmar#39211
7 International Crisis Group, *Asia Report No. 251: The Dark Side of Transition: Violence Against Muslims in Myanmar*, October 1 2013, https://d2071andvip0wj.cloudfront.net/the-dark-side-of-transition-violence-against-muslims-in-myanmar.pdf
8 Michael Jerryson, "Buddhist Traditions and Violence", in *The Oxford Handbook of Religion and Violence*, eds. Mark Juergensmeyer, Margo Kitts and Michael Jerryson (Oxford: Oxford University Press, 2013), 42.
9 Irm Haleem, *The Essence of Islamist Extremism: Recognition through Violence, Freedom through Death* (London: Routledge, 2012), 36.
10 Katie Hunt, "How Myanmar's Buddhists actually feel about the Rohingya," *CNN News*, 20 September, 2017, https://edition.cnn.com/2017/09/19/asia/myanmar-yangon-rohingya-buddhists/index.html
11 Haleem, *The Essence of Islamist Extremism*, 97.
12 Ibid.
13 Ibid., 135.
14 Ibid.
15 Ivan Watson, "Anti-Muslim tension simmers ahead of Myanmar election," *CNN News*, 3 November, 2015.
16 Peter A. Coclanis, "Terror in Burma: Buddhists vs Muslims", *World Affairs* 176:4 (2013), 30.
17 Michael Jerryson, "Buddhists and Violence: Historical Continuity/Academic Incongruities", *Religion Compass* 95 (2015), 141–150.
18 Usaid Siddiqui, "Muslim Minorities in Peril: The Rise of Buddhist VIolence in Asia," *Al Jazeera Centre for Studies*, 8 September, 2016, http://studies.aljazeera.net/en/reports/2016/09/muslim-minorities-peril-rise-buddhist-violence-asia-160908090547506.html
19 David Frankfurter, "The Construction of Evil and the Violence of Purification", in *The Oxford Handbook of Religion and Violence*, eds. Mark Juergensmeyer, Margo Kitts and Michael Jerryson (Oxford: Oxford University Press, 2013), 521–532.
20 "Five Precepts of Buddhism Explained", Edward Conze, Tricycle Magazine, accessed May 1, 2018, https://tricycle.org/magazine/the-five-precepts/
21 "The History, Philosophy, and Practice of Buddhism", Buddha101.com, accessed May 1, 2018, https://buddha101.com/
22 Jerryson, "Buddhists and Violence: Historical Continuity/Academic Incongruities", 14.
23 Marella Oppenheim, "It Only Takes One Terrorist: The Buddhist Monk Who Reviles Myanmar's Muslims", *The Guardian*, May 12, 2017, www.theguardian.com/global-development/2017/may/12/only-takes-one-terrorist-buddhist-monk-reviles-myanmar-muslims-rohingya-refugees-ashin-wirathu

24 “Racist Leader Monk Rev. Wirathu’s Speech”, Muang Zarni, M-Media Group, accessed May 1, 2018, www.m-mediagroup.com/en/archives/7625
25 Frankfurter, “The Construction of Evil”, 527.
26 Ibid., 526.
27 Mark Juergensmeyer and Mona Kanwal Sheikh, “A Sociotheological Approach to Understanding Religious Violence”, in *The Oxford Handbook of Religion and Violence*, eds. Mark Juergensmeyer, Margo Kitts and Michael Jerryson (Oxford: Oxford University Press, 2013), 521–532.
28 Bernard Cheah, “Is Facebook Myanmar’s Newest Daily?”, *Southeast Asian Press Alliance*, January 22 2016, www.seapa.org/is-facebook-myanmars-newest-daily/
29 Annie Gowen and Max Bearak, “Fake News on Facebook Fans the Flames of Hate against the Rohingya in Burma”, *The Washington Post*, December 8, 2017, www.washingtonpost.com/world/asia_pacific/fake-news-on-facebook-fans-the-flames-of-hate-against-the-rohingya-in-burma/2017/12/07/2c1fe830-ca1f-11e7-b506–8a10ed11ecf5_story.html?noredirect=on&utm_term=.902011d9e581
30 Daniel W. Kent, “Onward Buddhist Soldiers: Preaching to the Sri Lankan Army”, in *Buddhist Warfare*, eds. Michael K. Jerryson and Mark Juergensmeyer (Oxford: Oxford University Press, 2010), 162.
31 Quintan Wiktorowicz, “Introduction: Islamic Activism and Social Movement Theory”, in *Islamic Activism: A Social Movement Theory Approach*, ed. Quintan Wiktorowicz (Bloomington: Indiana University Press, 2004), 1–36.
32 John Hall, “Religion and Violence from a Sociological Perspective”, in *The Oxford Handbook of Religion and Violence*, eds. Mark Juergensmeyer, Margo Kitts and Michael Jerryson (Oxford: Oxford University Press, 2013), 363–374.
33 Pamela Stewart and Andrew Strathern, “Religion and Violence from an Anthropological Perspective”, in *The Oxford Handbook of Religion and Violence*, eds. Mark Juergensmeyer, Margo Kitts and Michael Jerryson (Oxford: Oxford University Press, 2013), 375–384.
34 Max Fisher, “Myanmar, Once a Hope for Democracy, Is Now a Study in How It Fails”, *The New York Times*, October 9, 2017, www.nytimes.com/2017/10/19/world/asia/myanmar-democracy-rohingya.html
35 Jonah Fisher, “Burma riots: Footage shows anti-muslim violence,” *BBC News*, 22 April, 2013, www.bbc.com/news/av/world-asia-22243438/burma-riots-footage-shows-anti-muslim-violence

5 Legalisation of violence against the Pakistani Ahmadis

Abdul Basit

Since the Afghan Jihad in the 1980s, Pakistani society has become progressively intolerant and conservative, where the tendency to settle religious disputes through violence has increased. This culture of violence involving religion has emboldened the traditional Islamists[1] and violent-extremist groups[2] to expand their influence and squeeze the already narrow space for the religious minorities in the country, particularly the heterodox minority sect, the Ahmadiyya.[3]

Coupled with this, the laws and policies adopted by the Pakistani state in 1974 (Second Constitutional Amendment) and 1984 (Ordinance XX of the Pakistan Penal Code), which ex-communicated the Ahmadis from Islam and criminalised their religious practices, have curbed their religious freedom. Since then, political marginalisation and social exclusion of the Ahmadis has continued at both the state and societal level. In Pakistan, Ahmadis are considered heretics and hence *Wajibul Qatal* (worthy of being killed) by some radical Islamists. Various forms of Ahmadis' persecution in Pakistan include public harassment, boycott of their businesses, targeted assassinations of influential Ahmadi figures and attacks on their worship places. This has forced the Ahmadis to seek asylum in the west or live in segregated neighbourhoods in Pakistan.

Against this backdrop, this chapter examines the ostracisation of the Ahmadis in Pakistan, contending that the state-led legalisation of the Ahmadis' ex-communication normalised violence against them resulting in growth and expansion of violent- extremism in the country. Furthermore, the anti-Ahmadi laws have fostered an environment of inequality privileging the mainstream Muslims over the Ahmadis in Pakistan.

Various military and civilian regimes in Pakistan institutionalised the anti-Ahmadi laws to appease the religious right for: (1) political survival, (2) to neutralise political competition from the religious-political parties and (3) to bolster their weak legitimacy. Unfortunately, the enactment of such laws did not stop at the Ahmadis. Following such appeasements, the state had to concede more space to the religious right along with the demands by the Sunni extremist groups to ex-communicate the Shias from Islam as well.

Divided in three sections, this chapter first looks at the demonisation of the Ahmadiyya community in Pakistan. Then it examines the de-jure and de-facto legalisation of Ahmadis' ex-communication and why, in the majority-minority construction of religious relations, Pakistan has suppressed the Ahmadiyya community. The final section looks at the wider implications of this trend for Pakistan's inter- and intra-faith harmony.

Demonisation of the Ahmadis

The Ahmadiyya movement, which emerged in the Indian sub-continent in 1889 and shifted to Pakistan after the partition, advocates reforms in Islam based on reasoning and logic as opposed to dogmatic and literalist interpretation of the traditional *ulama* (religious scholars).[4] Opposing blind-deference to traditional clerics, the Ahmadis believe in a rational interpretation of the Quran keeping the requirement and context of the present time in view. They also profess a metaphorical understanding of the second coming of the Christ and a non-violent approach to jihad.[5] Moreover, they adopt an innovative approach of engaging with the European philosophical debates to learn from other traditions and exhibit openness towards the west.[6]

Such reformist views undermine the traditional understanding of the Islamic doctrines as practiced by mainstream Muslims in Pakistan. Therefore, the Ahmadis are considered heretics and the founder of the movement, Ghulam Ahmed Mirza, is viewed as an imposter and a false prophet.[7] During Pakistan's formative years, a large number of the Ahmadis hailed from the educated-professional class. Hence, compared to their low numbers, the Ahmadis were disproportionately well represented at top government and administration positions in Pakistan (because of their education, not faith).[8]

This created insecurity among Pakistan's religious right, which viewed it as an attempt to increase the influence of the Ahmadi community in the country and launched an aggressive anti-Ahmadi campaign. As a result, the Ahmadi intake in government jobs declined, those who were already in service left and many were forced to resign from their jobs. In the business sector, the religious right made a nexus with trade unions to boycott the Ahmadi shops across Pakistan.[9] Fatwas were issued that doing business with the Ahamdis was *haram* (unlawful).

The persecution of the Ahmadis in Pakistan can be explained through American political scientist and expert of international and comparative law Christopher M. Larkin's model of politically judicialized governance, in which the probability of violence remains low as long as the state remains neutral in a triadic setting between any two rival ethnic, political or religious groups.[10]

On the contrary, when the state becomes partial by tilting towards one side or becomes indifferent, the probability of violence increases.[11]

In the context of Ahmadis' persecution in Pakistan, their overall situation was relatively better as long as the state maintained a position of neutrality. However, in 1974, these dynamics changed for the worst when the state dropped its neutrality as a triadic entity and moved from a position of guarantor of a dyadic relationship to a position tilting towards the religious right by officially declaring the Ahmadis as non-Muslims. This legalisation of the Ahmadis' ex-communication institutionalised discrimination and violence against them.[12]

In 1984, General Ziaul Haq further strengthened this legal apartheid by criminalising the worship and preaching of the Ahmadi faith by introducing Ordinance XX in the PPC. Since then, these two laws have become legal instruments of subjugation and suppression against the Ahmadis. Additionally, in most cases involving persecution of the Ahmadis, the state has acted either as an indifferent onlooker or it has been guilty of negligence or association.

Religious and political justifications for demonisation

Studies have shown that Muslim-majority states like Pakistan have a lacklustre record of religious freedom and harmony.[13] Pakistan consistently features quite high in indices of religious persecution. For instance, in Pew's Government Restriction Index, Pakistan is among the top states with very high restriction on religious freedom.[14] Likewise, as of July 2017, Pakistan ranked second among the countries which practise the grossest violation of international standards when it comes to religious freedom and where the "blasphemers" can face death.[15] On the Social Hostility Index 2015, Pakistan ranked 10th among the countries known for religious-violence and persecution.[16]

The persecution of the Ahmadis in Pakistan can be explored at two levels, religious and political. The orthodox Islamic groups ran an anti-Ahmadi campaign and advocated ruthless policies against them to retain their religious influence among their followers. Meanwhile, successive civilian and military regimes in Pakistan have appeased the religious-political parties for regime survival, to overcome the competition posed by the religious-political parties and to perpetuate their rule.[17]

Religious factors

Right after its creation, Pakistan's quest for Islamic nationalism as opposed to Hindu India gave more space to religion in the constitution-making and policy-formulation process. It is in this context that the Ahmadiyya community came in the crosshairs of Pakistan's religious right and the project of Islamic nationalism inadvertently turned into Sunni majoritarianism that discriminated against other Islamic minority sects and religious communities.[18]

Arguably, the Ahmadis' reformist and progressive interpretation of Islam undermined the traditional understanding of the Islamic doctrine practiced by orthodox Muslim groups in Pakistan and posed a stronger competition for the Islamists.[19] Besides, the Ahmadis' flexible and progressive approach made them popular among the urban-professional class. This bred insecurity among the Pakistani Islamists who demanded strict laws and policies to curb Ahmadis' religious freedom. Typically, orthodox religious groups tend to be rigid and status-quo-oriented as opposed to new and reformist groups which are innovative and progressive. This can lead to a conflict of interest between majority and minority religious groups. Consequently, the group belonging to the dominant faith paints the minority faith as evil (enemies of Islam, agents of the west, infidels in this case).[20]

Another possible reason for ruthless opposition and discrimination against the Ahmadis by Pakistan's religious right could be its poor electoral-performance in the parliamentary elections. Religious-political parties in Pakistan have never won any parliamentary election; they have either remained political-pressure groups or junior coalition partners in provincial government in the smaller provinces (Khyber Pakhtunkhwa and Baluchistan).[21] One effective way of shoring up political support was to use the slogan of "Islam is in danger" and the Ahmadis were the perfect scapegoat for being so-called enemies of Islam and agents of the west.

Political factors

Since its creation, Pakistan never had a stable political order and as a result, democracy as a system of governance could not take roots in the country. For more than half of its national life, Pakistan has witnessed four military rules. Due to weak democratic culture, the civilian governments (considered incompetent and corrupt) and the military regimes (viewed as power usurpers) had a very weak legitimacy base leaving them vulnerable to popular dissent. To bolster their weak legitimacy, they co-opted the Islamists by granting them various concessions.[22]

In traditional Muslim societies, if a regime enjoys good relations with the Islamic clergy, it is likely to have a good reputation among the masses. On the contrary, an unpopular regime deemed soft on religious minorities can swiftly lose support in countries like Pakistan. So, the successive governments in Pakistan have appeased the religious right to stay on the right side of public opinion.

For instance, when Zulfiqar Ali Bhutto declared the Ahmadis as non-Muslims, he was facing public backlash for failure to deliver on his election promises of economic development (roti, kapra aur makaan). He was also unpopular among the democratic forces that were disillusioned by his autocratic and centralised style of ruling.[23] At the same time, a coalition of traditional religious groups and Islamist parties spearheaded by Maulana Maududi of Jmaate Islami was running a nationwide anti-Ahmadi campaign instigating violence against the Ahmadis and demanding that they be relegated to a status of the apostate. The protesters threatened to overthrow the government if the Ahmadis were not declared as non-Muslims. To save his government in the face of declining legitimacy and popularity (regime survival) and to neutralise the political competition from the anti-Ahmadi Islamist groups, Bhutto passed the Second Constitutional Amendment declaring the Ahmadis officially as non-Muslims.[24]

Similarly, General Ziaul Haq heavily depended on the religious-political parties for political legitimacy and power perpetuation. He introduced Ordinance XX in the PPC, Hudood Ordinance, and the Blasphemy Laws that have benefited the religious-political parties and created a hostile environment for the religious minorities.[25]

Likewise, when General Musharraf took power in October 1999, he was viewed as a liberal and progressive leader. Initially, Musharraf made all the right political noises of dismantling the terrorist networks, reforming the Blasphemy Laws, improving the situation of the religious minorities and promoting enlightened moderation in Pakistan. However, he faltered on his commitment to reforms under popular pressure from the opposition of the Muttahida Majlis Amal (MMA), the six-party alliance of religious political parties.[26] For instance, in 2002, Musharraf introduced the electoral reforms bill removing the separate electoral policies for the religious minorities, which restricted their right to franchise only for the candidates of their own community. Removing this bar allowed the minority communities to vote like other normal Pakistani citizens. The MMA framed this as a move to mainstream the Ahmadis and compromising on the issue of Khatme Nabuwat (finality of the Prophethood) forcing Musharraf to retain the condition of separate electoral rule for the Ahmadis.[27]

Legal justification for demonisation

The state-approved anti-Ahmadi laws and policies remain the primary source of sectarian dispute and religiously inspired violence in Pakistan.[28] The anti-Ahmadi legalisation is of two types, de-jure or direct legalisation and de-facto or indirect legalisation.

De-jure legalisation

Direct legalisation of the Ahmadis' persecution is codified in the Second Constitutional Amendment Act, 1974 and the Ordinance XX, 1984 of the Pakistan Penal Code (PPC). With these amendments, the Ahmadis essentially became the only minority sect whose persecution was officially approved by the state. Bhutto's capitulation to and appeasement of the religious right marked a watershed movement in Pakistan's chequered constitutional history with far-reaching consequences on the Islamist politics in the country as well as inter- and intra-faith harmony in Pakistan, which became polarised and violent.

The Second Amendment became part of the 1973 Constitution on September 7, 1974, and declared the Ahmadis as non-Muslims. In Article 260, after clause (2), the following new clause (3) was introduced:

> A person who does not believe in the absolute and unqualified finality of The Prophethood of Muhammad (Peace be upon him), the last of the Prophets or claims to be a Prophet, in any sense of the word or of any description whatsoever, after Muhammad (Peace be upon him), or recognises such a claimant as a Prophet or religious reformer, is not a Muslim for the purposes of the Constitution or law.[29]

To date, various forms of religiously inspired violence in Pakistan draw legitimacy from this law. The ex-communication of the Ahmadis from Islam became the primary theological justification for killing them. It created a permissible environment for violence, discrimination and segregation against the Ahmadis. In other words, the extremist and sectarian groups were the direct beneficiary of this law.

The plight of the Ahmadis did not stop at their declaration as non-Muslims. In 1984, military ruler General Ziaul Haq went a step further and criminalised preaching of the Ahmadi beliefs and acts of worship. Section 298-B and 298-C of the PPC, introduced by the Zia regime, barred the Ahmadis from calling their places of worship as a masjid (mosque), preaching of their faith or distribution of their religious literature, reciting the call to prayer (azaan), referring to themselves as a Muslim or pose as a Muslim. Section 298-B of the PPC notes:

> Any person of the Qadiani group (who call themselves "Ahmadis" or by any other name) who by words, either spoken or written, or by visible representation, refers to, or address, any person, other than a Caliph or companion of the Holy Prophet (Peace Be Upon Him), as "Ameer-ul-Mominenn", "Khalifat-ul-Mumineen", "Khalifat-ul-Muslimeen", "Sahaabi", or "Razi Allah Anho"; refers to, or address, any person,

> other than the wife of the Holy Prophet (Peace Be Upon Him), as "Ummul Mumineen"; refers to, or address, any person, other than a member of the family "Ahle bait"; or refers to, or names, or calls, his place of worship as "Masjid"; shall be punished with imprisonment of either description of a term which may extend to three years, and shall also be liable to fine.[30]

Section 298-C notes:

> Any person of the Qadiani or Lahori group (who call themselves as "Ahmadis" or by any other name) who by words, either spoken or written, or by visible representation refers to the mode or form of call to prayers followed by his faith as "Azan", or recites Azan as used by the Muslim, shall be punished with imprisonment of either description of a term which may extend to three years, and shall also be liable to fine.[31]

Since the enactment of Ordinance XX, there have been as many as 120 attacks on Ahmadis' worship places across Pakistan. Additionally, over 250 Ahmadis have been killed in religiously motivated targeted assassinations. The conviction rate of murder cases involving the Ahmadis' killing is abysmally low, less than 1%. Killing the Ahmadis is risk-free for the assassins because the law-enforcement agencies adopt an indifferent attitude and as a result, most of the killers are acquitted in these cases.

According to a report, as many as 765 cases have been registered against the members of the Ahmadi community for displaying kalim and 447 cases for posing as Muslims since 1984. Similarly, around 161 Ahmadis have been booked for using Islamic epithets and another 806 for preaching the Ahmadi beliefs in Pakistan.[32]

De-facto legalisation

Besides the previously mentioned constitutional laws, there is a compendium of prosecution laws such as the blasphemy sections of the PPC, institutionalisation of certain Islamic Rules and the Separate Electoral Policies that indirectly or in de-facto manner legalise discrimination and political disenfranchisement of the Ahmadis relegating them to a status of second-grade citizens.

In 1985, as part of his Islamisation policies, Ziaul Haq introduced a separate electoral policy for the religious minorities. Before the separate electoral system, all the registered voters irrespective of their religion could vote for any eligible candidate of their choice in Pakistan. Similarly, the candidates could run for elections notwithstanding their religious background.

With the introduction of the separate electoral policy, a separate electoral register was created for the minorities, which mandated them to declare their religion before casting their ballot, and then were given a ballot accordingly. The separate electoral policy barred them from voting for the candidates running in the general elections except for those from their own community.[33] This policy particularly discriminated against the Ahmadis because it necessitated that, in order to vote, they had to declare themselves as non-Muslim (see the discussion on the separate electoral policies under "Political Factors").

Similarly, the institutionalisation of particular Islamic laws indirectly discriminates against the Ahmadis and other religious minorities by privileging the Muslims over them.[34] In areas such as the head of state eligibility, apostasy and family disputes involving Muslim and a member of religious minorities, these laws adopt a standard that goes to the advantage of the Muslims. Thus, these laws advance an inequality between Muslims and religious minorities though they do not curb the religious freedom of the minorities in a direct manner.[35]

For instance, as per the law, a non-Muslim is not eligible to become the head of the state (President). Similarly, the institutionalisation of such laws has fostered an environment in which members of the minorities are highly unlikely to hold a position of influence or authority in government. In cases of apostasy, while conversion to Islam by members of the minorities is welcomed, the conversion of a Muslim to any other religion is considered heretical and punishable by death. Likewise, in family disputes involving a Muslim and a member of religious minorities, the Islamic law takes precedence over the Family Law to the disadvantage of the minorities. Separately, before getting a passport, Muslims in Pakistan have to sign a declaration testifying that they do not consider the Ahmadis as Muslims.[36]

In 1986, the Ordinance XX was supplemented by the introduction of Blasphemy Laws that further reinforced the indirect pattern of discrimination against the Ahmadis and other religious minorities.[37] Given the vague language and procedural lacunas in the Blasphemy Laws, they have been grossly misused to prosecute the religious minorities and settle personal vendettas.[38] For instance, before the enactment of the Blasphemy Laws, only 14 cases of blasphemy were reported in Pakistan. However, after the enactment of the laws, between 1986 and 2007 around 647 people were charged with blasphemy charges, 50% of which were non-Muslims.[39]

Since the enactment of the Blasphemy Laws, the Majlise Tahafuze Khatme Nabuwat (MTKN), a conglomerate of anti-Ahmadi Islamist organisations, has used them as a legitimacy tool to oppress the Ahmadis. Using its street power, the MTKN has opposed any move to amend the Blasphemy Laws, painting them as an effort to secularise and westernise Pakistan.[40]

Hence, since the enactment of these laws, not a single move to amend them has succeeded.[41]

From the law-enforcement and prosecution perspective, there is tremendous social and ideological pressure on the police and judiciary that it is impossible for the two state organs to acquit a person in such cases even if he or she is innocent. There have been instances where extremist groups have attacked judges who have acquitted people in blasphemy cases. Moreover, even lawyers often refuse to defend a person accused of blasphemy due to intimidation and death threats.[42] Those who take up the cases are harassed or murdered. For instance, human rights lawyer Rashid Rehman was murdered in May 2014 for representing the case of academic Junadi Hafeez, a lecturer from Bahauddin Zakariya University, accused of blasphemy.[43]

Final reflections

Pakistan's decision to ex-communicate the Ahmadis at the official level by caving to the religious rights' demands has normalised and legalised violence against them. Various Pakistani governments did this to neutralise the political competition from religious groups, for ideological legitimisation or power perpetuation. Various extremist groups have used the Ahmadi-specific laws introduced in the constitution and they are structural impediments in removing discrimination against the hapless community in Pakistan. Overall, Pakistan's plural religious ethos has been seriously damaged.

Notes

1 Traditional Islamist groups are those which practice Islamist politics and activism without engaging in violence. These groups use the anti-Ahamdi laws in Pakistan as a tool for political mobilisation. Such groups include Jamate Islami (JI), Jamiate Ulame Islam Fazal Group (JUI-F), Tehrike Khatme Nabuwat (TKN), Sunni Tehrik (ST), Sunni Ittehad Council (SIC), Tehreek-e-Labbaik Ya Rasool Allah (TLY), et al.

2 Violent-extremist groups are those which engage in vigilante and militant violence using the anti-Ahamdi laws as ideological justification for their acts of terrorism. Such groups include Al-Qaeda, Tehrik-e-Taliban Pakistan (TTP), Lashkar-e-Jhangvi (LeJ), Jamaat-ul-Ahrar (JuA), the Islamic State of Khurasan (ISK), Jaish-e-Muhammad (JeM), et al.

3 In Pakistan, the members of the Ahmadiyya community are referred to as the Ahmadis. Derogatorily, they are also called Mirzais (followers of Mirza Ghulam Ahmad, the founder of the Ahmadiyya movement) and Qadyanis (Qadyan is a place in India where the Ahmadiyya movement was born).

4 "The Ahmadiyya: Beliefs and Practices", *Reason on Faith*, June 9, 2016, accessed at http://reasononfaith.org/ahmadiyya-beliefs-and-practice/ on September 26, 2017.

5 Ibid.
6 Kunto Sofianto, "Mirza Ghulam Ahmad: Founder of the Ahmadiyya Muslim from Qadian, India", *International Journal for Historical Studies*, Vol. 7. No. 2, April 2016, pp. 183–200, accessed at www.academia.edu/28203392/Mirza_Ghulam_Ahmad_Founder_of_the_Ahmadiyya_Muslim_from_Qadian_India?auto=download on September 24, 2017.
7 "Who Are Ahmadis?", *BBC News*, May 28, 2010, accessed at http://news.bbc.co.uk/2/hi/south_asia/8711026.stm on September 25, 2017.
8 For instance, the leading commander of the Pakistan army in the 1965 war with India, Lieutenant General (Retired) Akhtar Malik, and the main hero of the fabled battle of tanks at Chawinda, Lieutenant General (Retired) Abdul Ali, were Ahmadis. Similarly, the noted Pakistani scientist and Nobel Laureate Dr. Abdul Salam is also an Ahmadi.
9 "A Report on Persecution of the Ahmadis in Pakistan during the Year 2016", p. 56, accessed at www.persecutionofahmadis.org/wp-content/uploads/2017/02/Persecution-of-Ahmadis-in-Pakistan-2016.pdf on September 20, 2017.
10 Christopher M. Larkins, "Independence and Democratization: A Theoretical and Conceptual Analysis", *The American Journal of Comparative Law*, Vol. 44, No. 4, Autumn, 1996, pp. 605–626.
11 Ibid.
12 Usman Ahmad, "Pakistan's Original Sin", *Foreign Policy*, October 13, 2014, accessed at http://foreignpolicy.com/2014/10/13/pakistans-original-sin/ on September 20, 2017.
13 Anugrah Kumar, "USCIRF Report Shows Islamic Countries Are Worst Violators of Religious Freedom: 12 Muslim-Majority Nations Top the List", *The Christian Post*, May 1, 2015, accessed at www.christianpost.com/news/uscirf-report-shows-islamic-countries-are-worst-violators-of-religious-freedom-12-muslim-majority-nations-top-the-list-138512/ on September 24, 2017.
14 "Trends in Global Restrictions on Religion", *Pew Research Centre*, June 23, 2016, accessed at www.pewforum.org/2016/06/23/trends-in-global-restrictions-on-religion/ on September 24, 2017.
15 "Ranking Countries by Their Blasphemy Laws", *The Economist*, August 13, 2017, accessed at www.economist.com/blogs/erasmus/2017/08/anti-religious-speech on September 15, 2017.
16 "Global Restrictions on Religion Rise Modestly in 2015, Reversing Downward Trend", *Pew Research Centre*, April 11, 2017, accessed at www.pewforum.org/2017/04/11/global-restrictions-on-religion-rise-modestly-in-2015-reversing-downward-trend/ on September 4, 2017.
17 Fatima Zainab Rahman, "State Restrictions on the Ahmadiyya Sect in Indonesia and Pakistan: Islam or Political Survival", *American Journal of Political Science*, Vol. 49, No. 3, 2014, pp. 408–422, accessed at www.tandfonline.com/doi/abs/10.1080/10361146.2014.934656 on September 24, 2017.
18 Rasul Baksh Rais, "Islamic Radicalism and Minorities in Pakistan", in *The Pakistan Paradox: Instability and Resilience*, Christophe Jaffrelot (ed.) (New York: Oxford University Press, 2015), p. 445.
19 Roger Ballard, p. 1.
20 David Frankfurter, "The Construction of Evil and the Violence of Purification", in *The Oxford Handbook of Religion and the Violence of Purification*, Michael Jerryson et al. (eds.) (New York: Oxford University Press, 2013), pp. 522–523.

21 Abdul Basit, "The Rise of the Far Right", *The News*, October 6, 2017, accessed at www.thenews.com.pk/print/234962-The-rise-of-the-far-right on October 6, 2017.
22 Farahnaz Ispahani, *Purifying the Land of the Pure: Pakistan's Religious Minorities* (New York: Oxford University Press, 2017), pp. 63–65.
23 Hussain Haqqani, *Pakistan between Mosque and Military* (Washington, DC: Carnegie Endowment for International Peace, 2005), p. 98.
24 Ibid.
25 Fatima Zainab Rahman, ibid.
26 Rana Tanveer, "Ahmadis Still Out of Electoral Process", *Express Tribune*, April 22, 2013, accessed at https://tribune.com.pk/story/538686/franchise-ahmadis-still-out-of-electoral-process/ on September 28, 2017.
27 "Minorities under Attack: Faith-Based Discrimination and Violence in Pakistan", *Human Rights Commission of Pakistan*, Report No 647, February 2015, p. 10, accessed at www.fidh.org/IMG/pdf/20150224_pakistan_religious_minorities_report_en_web.pdf on September 22, 2017.
28 Though, the anti-Ahmadi campaigns began before the partition of the Indian sub-continent but they became more prominent and gained impetus after the creation of Pakistan.
29 The Constitution of Pakistan, Second Amendment Act (1974), accessed at www.pakistani.org/pakistan/constitution/amendments/2amendment.html on October 8, 2017.
30 Pakistan Penal Code, Article 298-B, "Misuse of Epithets, Descriptions and Titles, etc., Reserved for Certain Holy Personages or Places", accessed at www.pakistani.org/pakistan/legislation/1860/actXLVof1860.html on October 8, 2017.
31 Pakistan Penal Code, Article 298-C, "Person of Quadiani Group, etc., Calling Himself a Muslim or Preaching or Propagating His Faith", accessed at www.pakistani.org/pakistan/legislation/1860/actXLVof1860.html on October 8, 2017.
32 "A Report of the Persecution of the Ahmadis during the Year 2016", p. 128, accessed at www.persecutionofahmadis.org/wp-content/uploads/2017/02/Persecution-of-Ahmadis-in-Pakistan-2016.pdf on September 27, 2017.
33 All the candidates running for office have to give a statement declaring their religious affiliation and renounce Mirza Ghulam Ahmad as a false prophet or self-declare as non-Muslim and opt for the separate ballot system.
34 Fatima Zainab Rahman, ibid.
35 Ibid.
36 Farahnaz Ispahani, ibid, pp. 170–172.
37 It is important to note that Blasphemy Laws do not directly apply to the Ahmadis. Moreover, the Blasphemy Laws do not apply to the non-Muslims. (In Islam, the punishment for blasphemy is not death.) In the Hanafi fiqh, a person becomes apostate by committing blasphemy and the punishment for apostasy in Islam is death. It is in this context that Ahmadis have consistently been persecuted through the misuse of Blasphemy Laws, framing them as heretics and blasphemers.
38 "On Trial: The Implementation of Pakistan's Blasphemy Laws", *International Commission of Jurists*, November 2015, p. 28, accessed at http://icj.wpengine.netdna-cdn.com/wp-content/uploads/2015/12/Pakistan-On-Trial-Blasphemy-Laws-Publications-Thematic-Reports-2015-ENG.pdf on September 24, 2017.
39 Ibid.

40 Arafat Mazhar, “The Untold Story of Blasphemy Laws”, *Dawn*, December 9, 2014, accessed at www.dawn.com/news/1149558 on September 24, 2017.
41 “As Good as Dead: The Impact of the Blasphemy Laws in Pakistan”, *Amnesty International Report*, 2016, p. 31, accessed at www.refworld.org/pdfid/585a41704.pdf on September 24, 2017.
42 “On Trial: The Implementation of Pakistan’s Blasphemy Laws”, ibid.
43 “Rights Advocate Rashid Rehman Khan Gunned Down in Multan”, *Dawn*, May 7, 2014, accessed at www.dawn.com/news/1104788 on September 24, 2017.

6 Some reflections

"Process" and "outcome" as simultaneous phenomenon

Irm Haleem

The chapters in this book reinforce the Kalyvasian assertion that while the "process" and "outcome" of violence are indeed distinct stages of violence, they can still, nonetheless, exist simultaneously with each other, and in fact often do. In other words, the mechanisms in the process of violence (the mobilization for violence, narratives of violence, and what I call "metaphysical" violence) both "precede and follow" the outcome of violence (actual incidences of physical violence).[1] A classic example of this dynamic is illustrated in the manner in which Hannah Arendt made sense of Adolf Eichmann's complicity in the monstrosities of the Nazi regime. According to Arendt, there may have been a time when Eichmann was ill at ease with the monstrosities he was put in charge of, but over time, she notes, he became comfortable with the *idea* of violence. We may understand this in terms of the fact that while Eichmann was indeed mobilized by Nazi rhetoric (violence as process), his full commitment to the Nazi worldview occurred sometime after Nazi rhetoric was actualized into Nazi policies (violence as outcome). To put it simply, an individual's commitment to violence may be created in the stage of the mobilization process of violence, where narratives of violence romanticize violence (justify and legitimize violence), but their commitment to violence may become strengthened through their actual involvement in physical violence (either as commanders or combatants). There may be several reasons for this, such as the morphing of the narratives of violence (the process of violence) to suit the particular stage of the outcome of violence (physical violence), and the deeper commitment to violence by participants in wars of sorts, due to both personal involvements in violence as well as personal stakes in the continuation of violence, which further make such participants perpetually receptive to narratives of violence. For example, Arendt argues that Eichmann's commitment to Nazi ideals was significantly fueled by Eichmann's desire for recognition and promotion within the ranks of the Nazi SS hierarchy, which allowed

Eichmann to present his monstrous actions as matters of moral imperative, thereby ironically himself reinforcing the narratives of the Nazi machinery.[2]

The interplay between the process and outcome of violence is illustrated in all of the chapters in this book. The case study of Japan offers a textbook example of the process of violence, prior to the onset of actual physical violence. Here, we see that the moralization of violence takes shape indirectly through narratives of the old glory days of imperial Japan, an era of yesteryears that was characterized by Shinto ultra-nationalism and its consequent imperialist policies of expansionism and conquest. Kumada argues that the Abe administration is working on both constitutional reforms as well as educational reforms to align them to a pre-war Japanese ideological and political outlook that fundamentally challenges the post-war pacifist constitution. To the extent that imperialism of yesteryears is being glorified, violence is being subtly glorified, as imperialism is nothing if not a glorification of all means to an end, even the means of violence and monstrosity.

The case of China illustrates the simultaneous occurrence of the process and outcome of violence. Here, we see that violence is both moralized and legalized through packaging it in terms of the imperatives of counterterrorism. Kam argues that the moralization of the violence that is inherent in China's counterterrorism policies in the Xinjiang province is further facilitated through religious, cultural, and social controls in Xinjiang province. Creating a meta-narrative through controlling different facets of society at once siphons the probability of critique and resistance, as well as packages such critique as treasonous, thereby further normalizing violence.

The case of Myanmar offers another classic example of the simultaneous interplay between process and outcome of violence. Here, Dhanaraj argues that the violence against Rohingya Muslims is normalized through narratives that both moralize and legalize violence against Rohingyas. This is done in a multi-dimensional manner: through presenting Rohingyas as the 'other', and as not even worthy of being accounted for in a government census, and therefore presenting violence against them as a security measure against external threats; through presenting Rohingyas as a security threat to the dominant Buddhist identity; and through the denials by the government of its role in the ethnic cleansing of Rohingyas. Here, narratives of violence exist parallel to the outcomes of violence, and both narratives and outcomes reinforce each other.

The case of Pakistan offers yet another classic example of the simultaneous interplay between process and outcome of violence. Here, Basit addresses the de facto and de jure legalization of violence in Pakistan when he analyzes the dynamics that have reinforced sectarian violence against the Ahmadi sectarian minority. He argues that legalization of violence, through government polices that reinforce the excommunication of Ahmadis, has functioned to reinforce Sunni extremist narratives against Ahmadis. This works to further create the space within which Sunni extremist groups can function and target members of the Ahmadi community in broad daylight, thereby further normalizing violence on both moral and legal grounds.

Broader reflections on the normalization of violence establish the fact that the phenomenon of the normalization of violence is not unique to any one country, region, or people. In analyzing Hannah Arendt's critique of the US involvement in the Vietnam War,[3] George Kateb notes "war provides a cover for anticonstitutionalism, which in turn intensifies the illusion that war is necessary and urgent".[4] This, argues Kateb, leads to a "thrilling sense of indefinite potentiality for transgression".[5] This means that the narratives of morality and legality that are used to justify the violations of constitutional protections and legal barriers to extremism are largely done in the name of national security or self-defense. We have seen in the chapters in this book that narratives of moral necessity and national security are indeed constructed to cast a veil on the most extreme manifestations of domestic policy (militarism, counterinsurgency, counterterrorism, sectarian exclusionism). These narratives are thus used to manufacture the enemy, and to manufacture mass consent for the use of violence against the designated enemy. The use of force with impunity, along with a targeting of a collective (the members of the group designated as the enemy), is therefore the outcome.

Here, a note on Jacques Derrida's unique critique of the American 'war on terror' is relevant. Derrida analogized the excessive use of force in the war on terror to an autoimmune disease.[6] In an autoimmune disease, it is the over-active immune system that ends up destroying the very body that it is intended to save and protect. In the case of overly aggressive counterterrorism policies, it is these very policies that end up retarding the security of the populace that it professes to protect, through aggressive (over-active) actions that only succeed in generating a downward spiral of action-reaction of violence and instability. W.J.T Mitchell analogizes this dynamic as 'cloning terror'.[7]

The tendency of aggressive policies to function with impunity points to the siphoning of critique of such policies, which underscores Arendt's notion of the imperative of judgment (critique), without which standards of "right" or "wrong", "moral" or "immoral" can never be challenged.[8] Indeed, it is the very absence of the right to critique that reinforces the view that the notions of morality and legality, as professed by the governing entity, are indeed legitimate and unanimous, which further normalizes violence. The siphoning of dissent and judgment on the efficacy of counterterrorist, counterinsurgent, or exclusionary policies, and the framing of such dissent and judgment as treasonous or blasphemous—as in the case of China,

Myanmar, and Pakistan—only works to further normalize violence as it gives the illusion that such policies are indeed unequivocal on both moral and legal grounds.

Notes

1 Stathis N. Kalyvas, *The Logic of Violence in Civil Wars* (New York: Cambridge University Press, 2006), p. 21.
2 See Arendt's analysis of Eichmann as the man that he was in *Eichmann in Jerusalem*.
3 See Arendt, "Lying in Politics", as cited in George Kateb, "Fiction as Poison", *Thinking in Dark Times: Hannah Arendt on Ethics and Politics*, edited by Roger Berkowitz, Jeffrey Katz, and Thomas Keenan (New York: Fordham University Press, 2010), p. 29.
4 George Kateb, "Fiction as Poison", *Thinking in Dark Times: Hannah Arendt on Ethics and Politics*, edited by Roger Berkowitz, Jeffrey Katz, and Thomas Keenan (New York: Fordham University Press, 2010), p. 29.
5 George Kateb, "Fiction as Poison", *Thinking in Dark Times: Hannah Arendt on Ethics and Politics*, edited by Roger Berkowitz, Jeffrey Katz, and Thomas Keenan (New York: Fordham University Press, 2010), p. 30.
6 See William John Thomas Mitchell's analysis of Derrida's autoimmunity metaphor in *Cloning Terror: The War of Images, 9/11 to the Present* (Chicago: The University of Chicago Press, 2011), pp. 44–54.
7 See William John Thomas Mitchell, *Cloning Terror: The War of Images, 9/11 to the Present* (Chicago: The University of Chicago Press, 2011).
8 See Hannah Arendt, *Lectures on Kant's Political Philosophy*, edited by Ronald Beiner (Chicago: The University of Chicago Press, 1992), pp. 97–101.

Index

For Product Safety Concerns and Information please contact our EU
representative GPSR@taylorandfrancis.com
Taylor & Francis Verlag GmbH, Kaufingerstraße 24, 80331 München, Germany

www.ingramcontent.com/pod-product-compliance
Lightning Source LLC
Chambersburg PA
CBHW050538270326
41926CB00015B/3291

* 9 7 8 1 0 3 2 0 8 7 8 4 9 *